Contents

Basic Answers	1
Intermediate Answers	46
Advanced Answers	90

Elementary Music Rudiments© 2023 by San Marco Publications. All rights reserved.

All right reserved. No part of this book may be reproduced in any form or by electronic or mechanical means including Information storage and retrieval systems without permission in writing from the author.

ISBN: 1-896499-51-1

Elementary Music Rudiments Basic Answers

Page 3, No 1.

B A G E F E D A B C G E
C G A G D F A B C F G A
B A E F C B C D F E G F
B D E C G F A G F C F D
A F D G B E C E F G A B

Page 3, No. 2

Page 4, No. 2

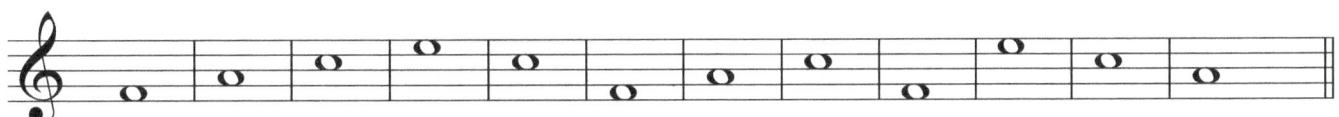
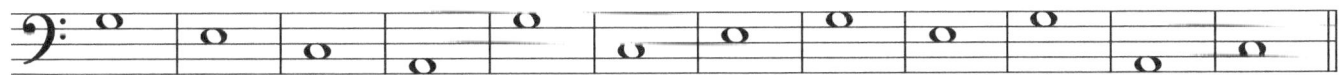

Page 5, No. 1

A E B F F E G F D C G E
A F C G A D B G C F G A
C F D G D G E A B A C G

Basic

Page 6, No. 2

Page 6, No. 3

Page 6, No. 4

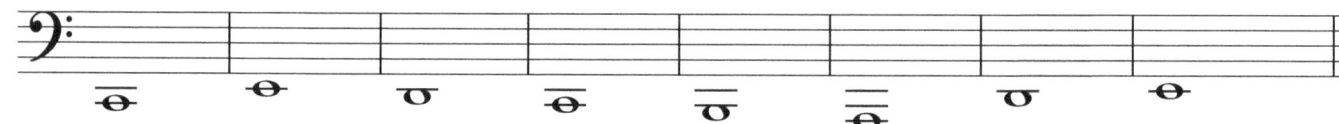

Page 6, No. 5

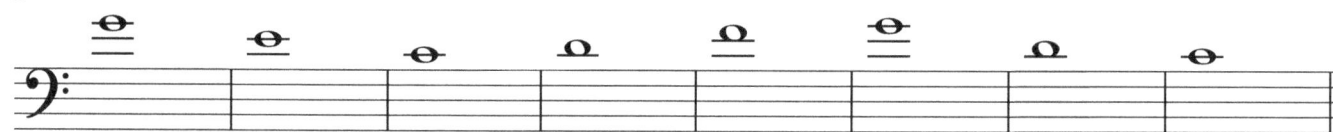

Page 6, No. 6

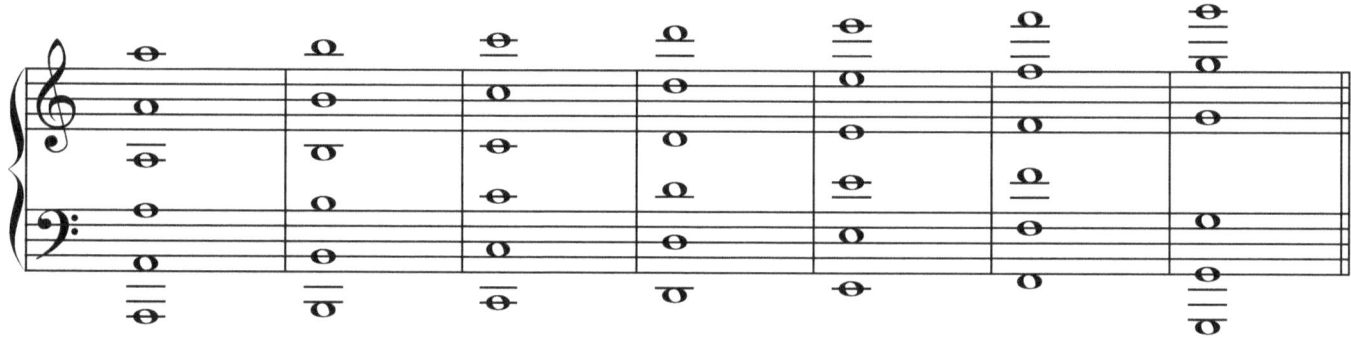

Page 9, No. 1

½	4	2
4	1	¼
3	¼	2
1½	¾	1

Page 11, No. 1

| whole note | quarter note | sixteenth note |
| dotted eighth note | eighth note | half note |

Basic

Page 11, No. 2

| sixteenth rest | quarter rest | half rest |
| whole rest | eighth rest | thirty-second rest |

Page 11, No. 3

Page 12, No. 4

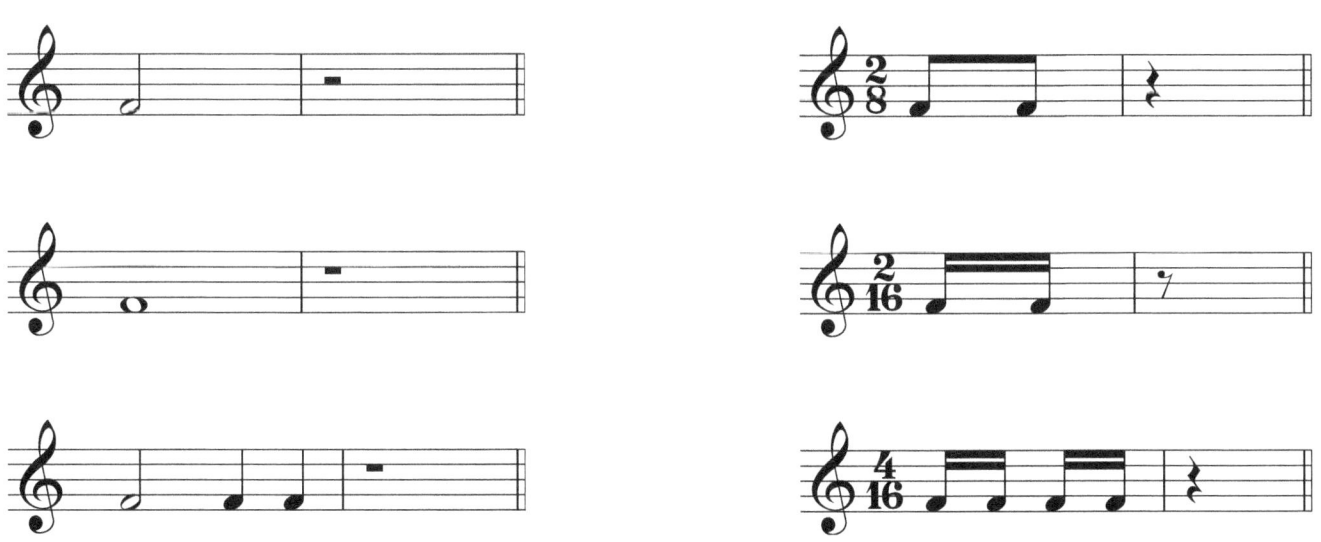

Basic

Page 12, No. 5

Page 12, No. 6

Page 13, No. 7

4
3
8
4
3
2
6
4
3

Basic

Page 13, No. 8

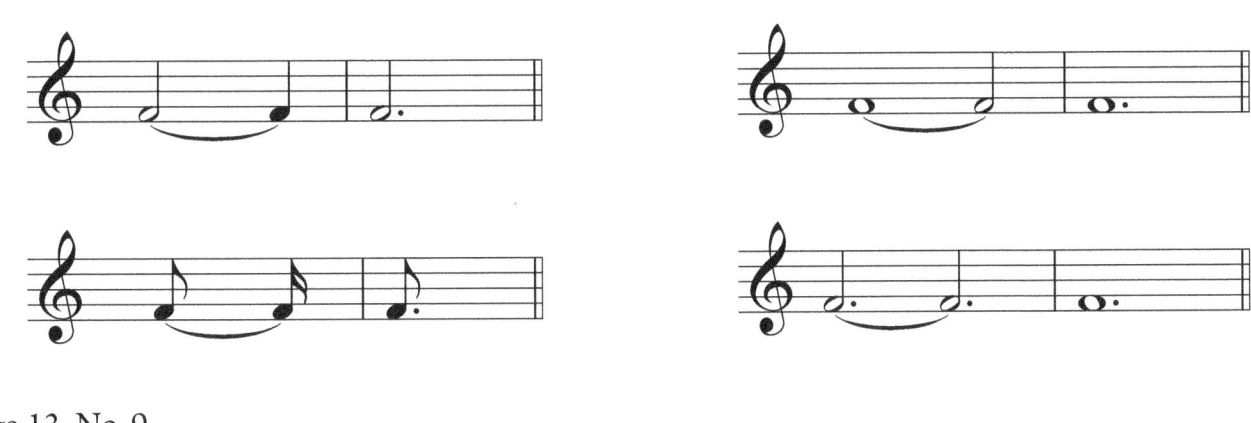

Page 13, No. 9

Page 14, No. 1 Review One

A	F	G	F	D	E	E	A	G	B
G	E	B	C	C	B	C	E	D	A
C	F	G	A	B	E	D	D	C	D
C	F	A	G	G	A	C	D	F	B

Page 15, No. 2

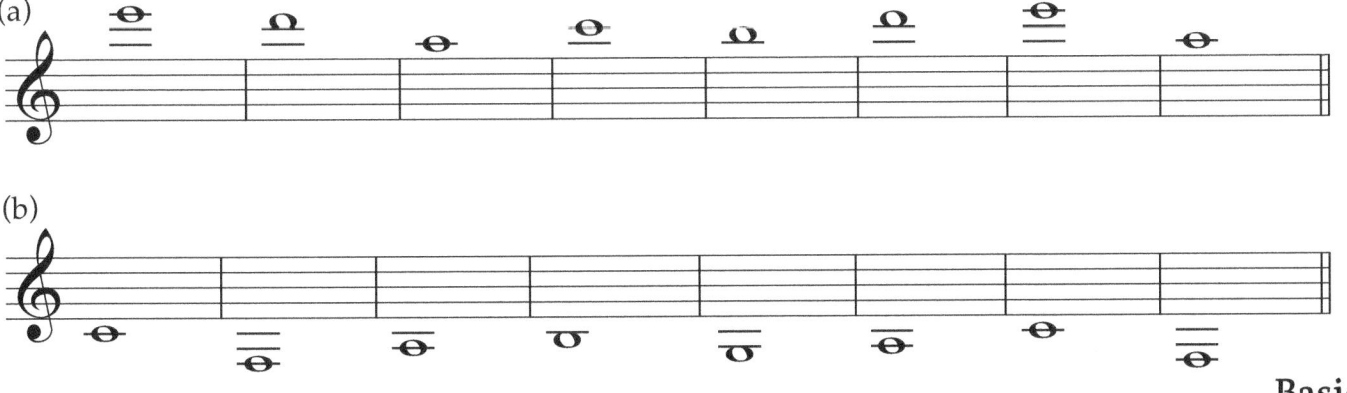

Basic

(c)

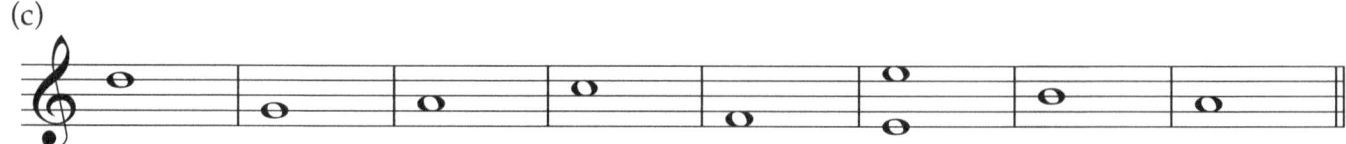

Page 15, No. 3

(a)

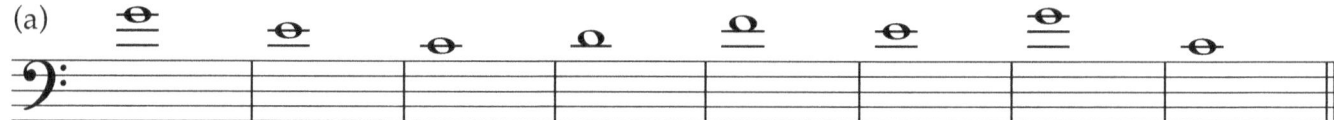

(b)

(c)

Page 16, No. 4

quarter rest	1 beat	whole note	4 beats
eighth rest	1/2 beat	sixteenth note	1/4 beat
eighth note	1/2 beat	sixteenth rest	1/4 beat
half note	2 beats	dotted half note	3 beats
whole note	4 beats	quarter note	1 beat
half rest	2 beats	whole rest	4 beats

Page 16, No. 5

Page 16, No. 6

Basic

Page 18, No. 1 (other options are possible)

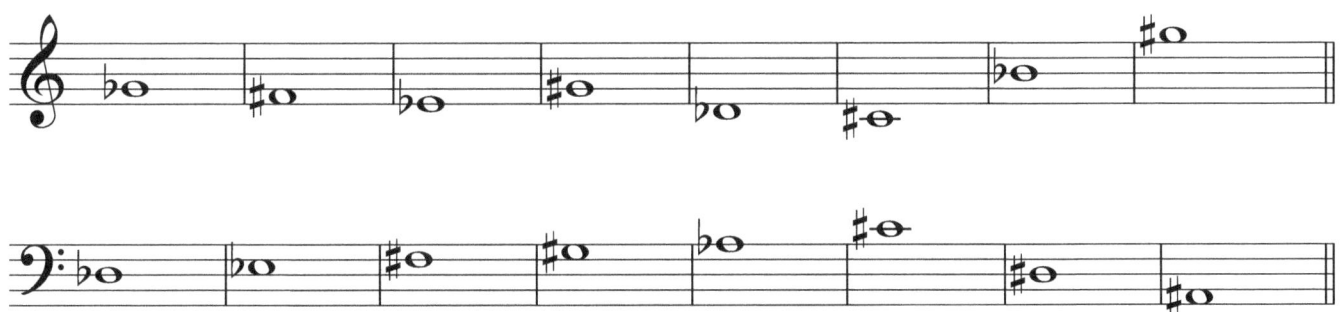

Page 19, No. 2

C W D C D C D W D C

Page 19, No. 3

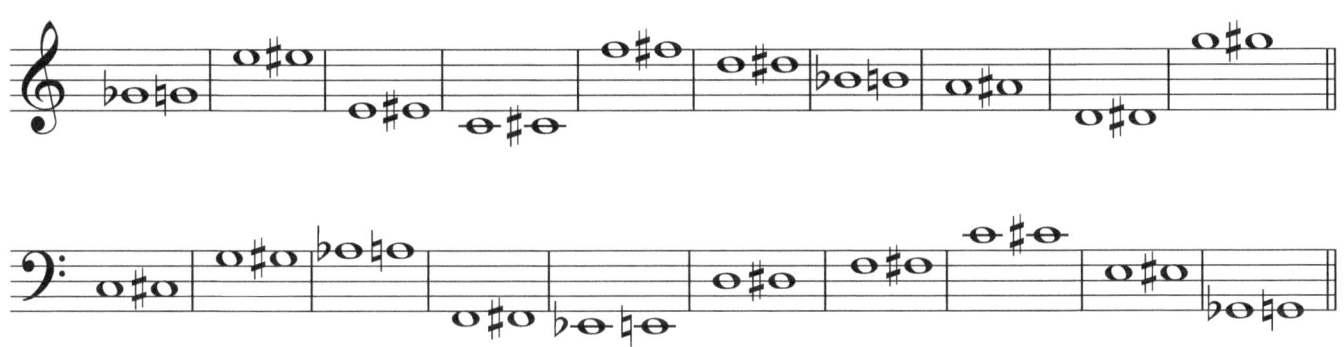

Page 19, No. 4

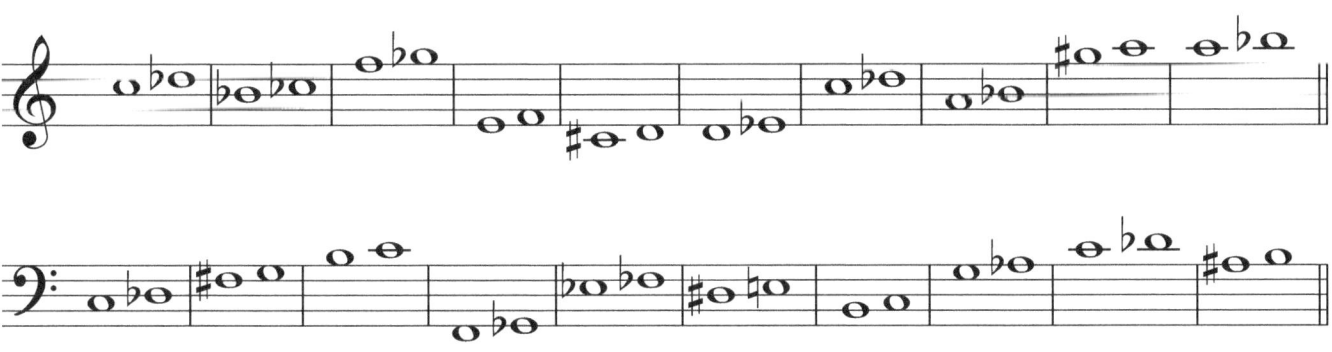

Basic

Page 20, No. 5

Page 20, No. 6

Page 20, No. 7

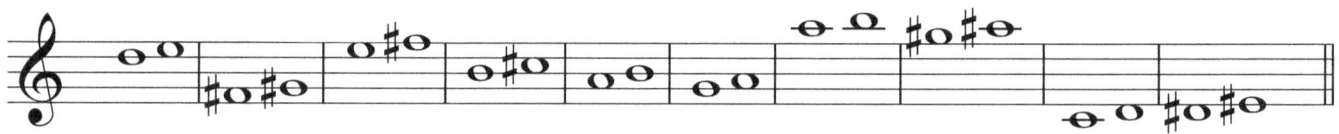

Page 20, No. 8

Page 20, No. 9

A♭ = G♯   G♯ = A♭   F♯ = G♭
B♭ = A♯   C♯ = D♭   E♭ = D♯

Basic

Page 25, No. 5

| D major | G major | A major | E major |
| E major | B♭ major | E♭ major | A♭ major |

Page 25, No. 6

B♭ E♭	F♯	F♯ C♯ G♯
F♯ C♯	B♭ E♭ A♭	B♭ E♭ A♭ D♭
B♭	F♯ C♯ G♯ D♯	none

Page 26, No. 1

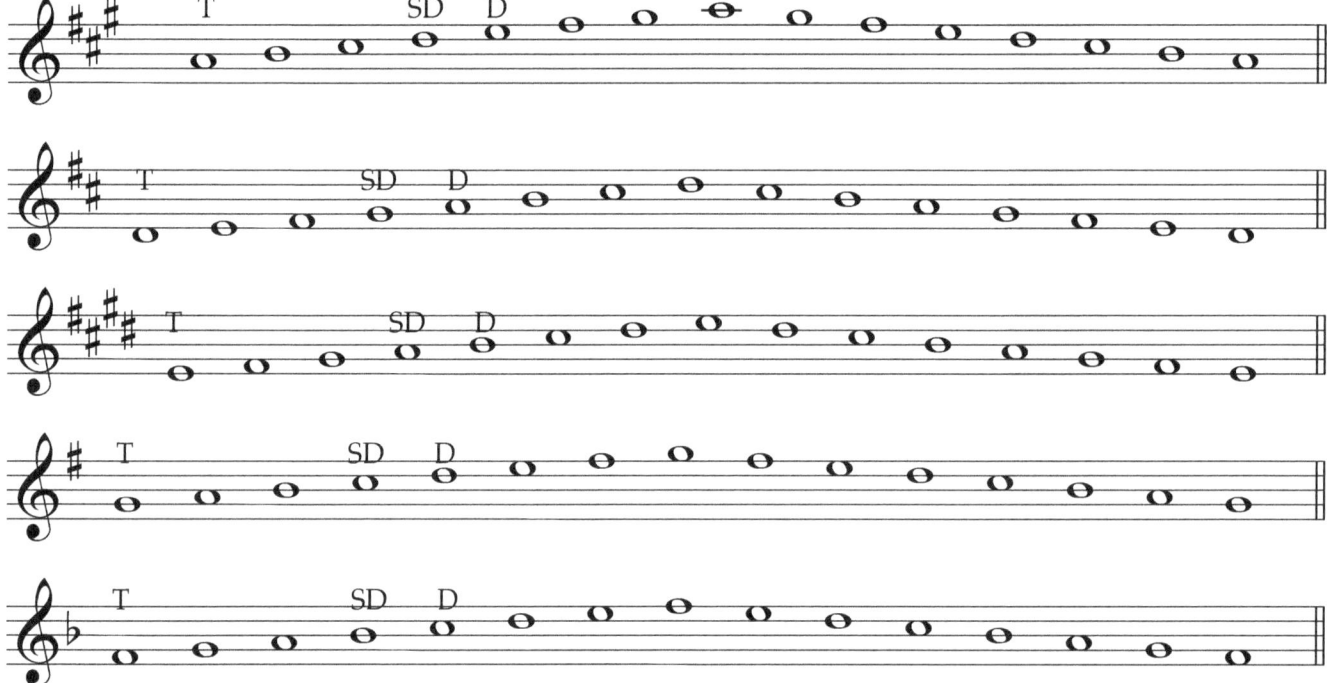

Page 27, No. 2

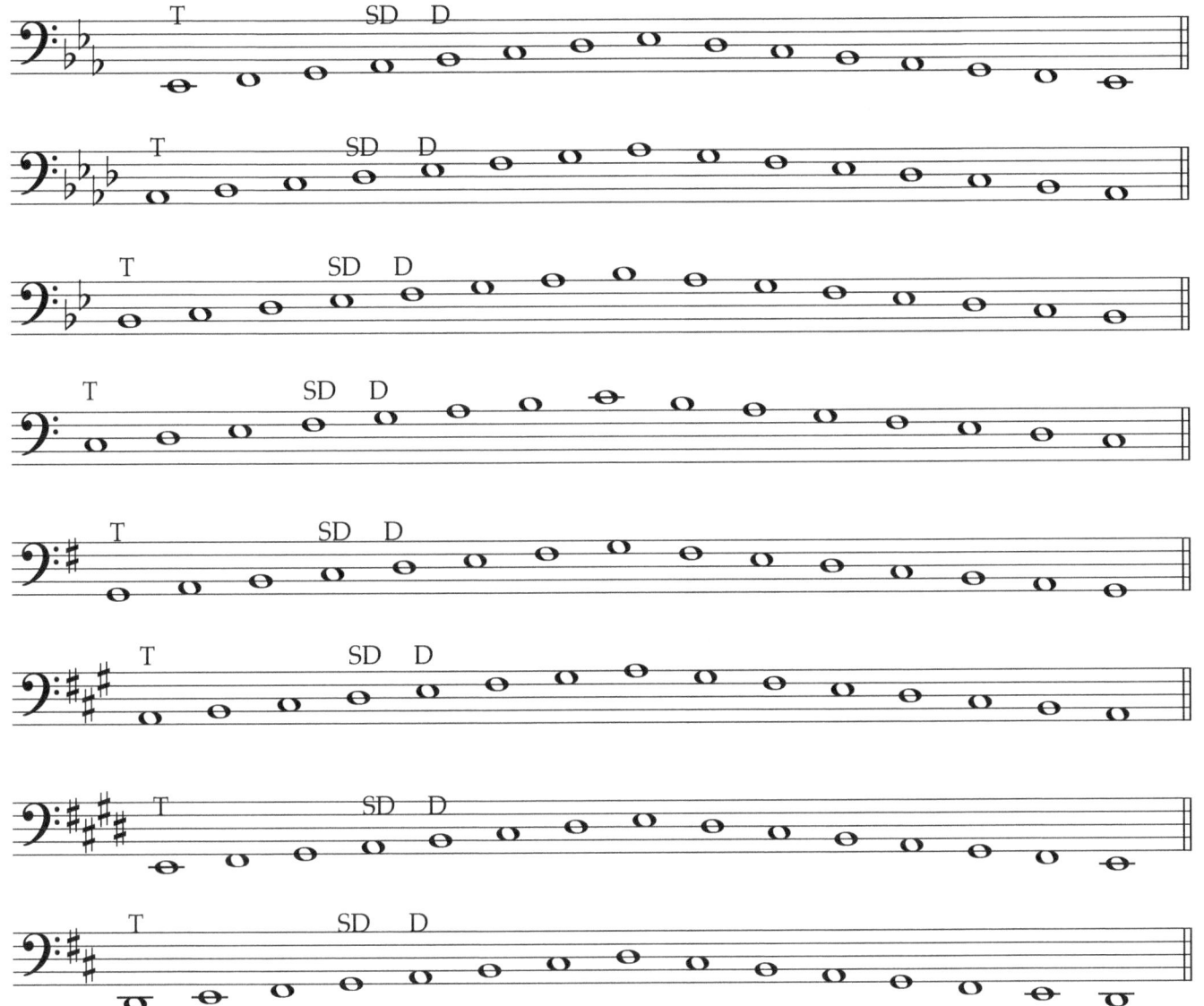

Page 28, No. 3

A major	F major	A♭ major	D major	B♭ major
T	D	SD	D	T

C major	G major	E♭ major	E major	D major
D	T	D	SD	D

Basic

Page 28 and 29, No. 4

Page 29, No. 5

Basic

Page 30, No. 6

Page 30, No. 7

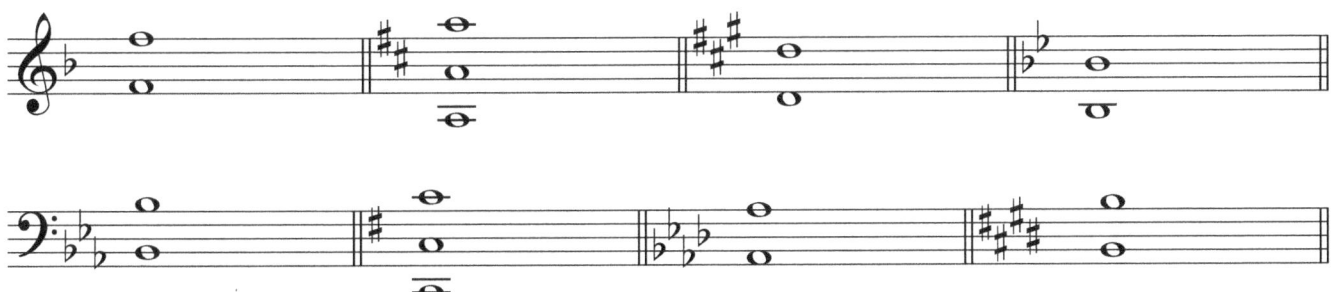

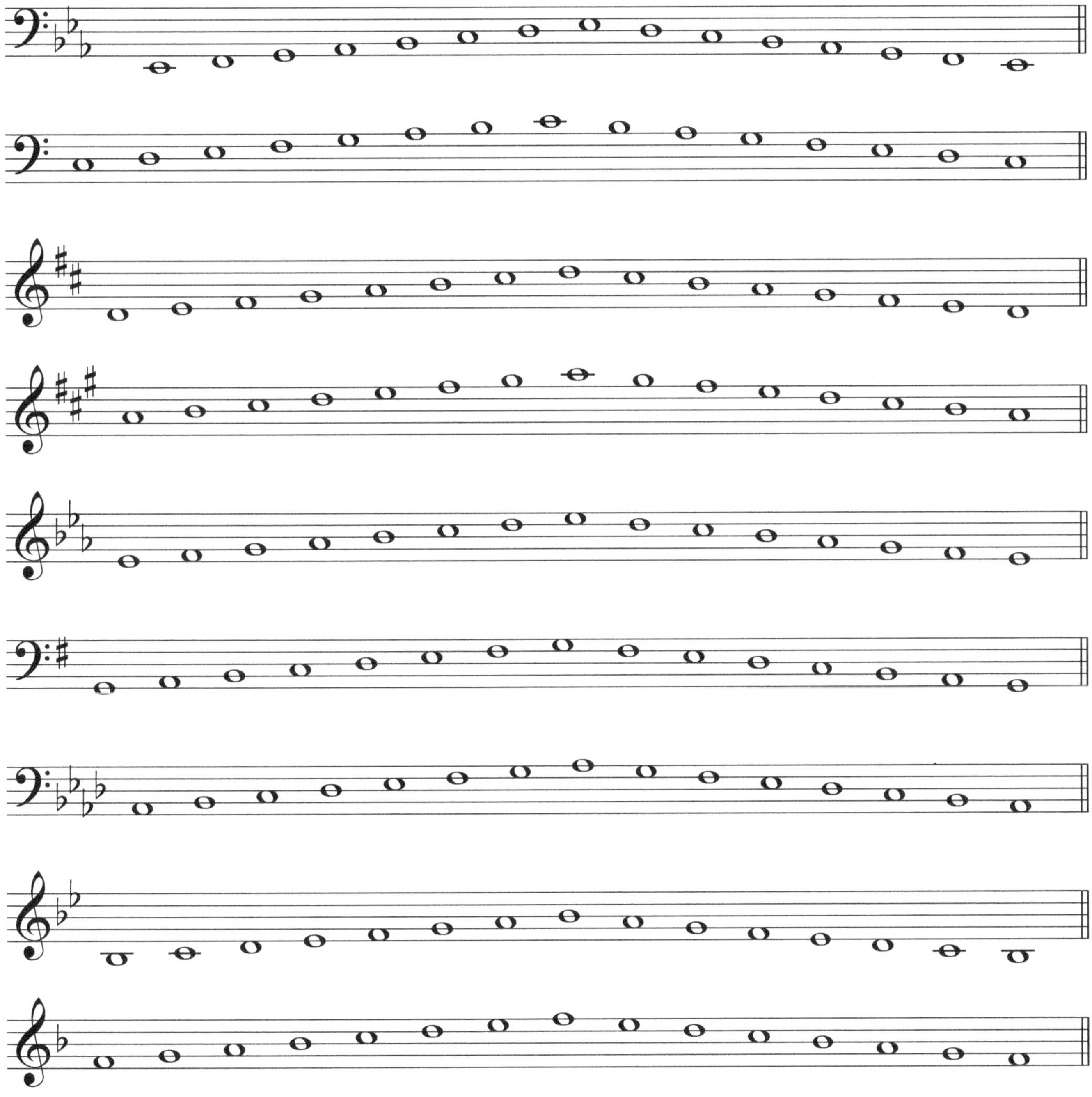

Page 32, No. 9

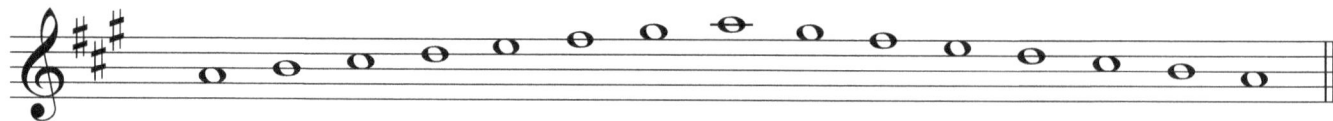

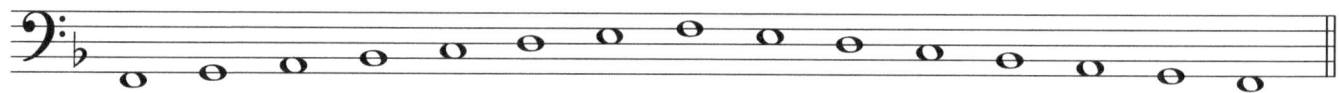

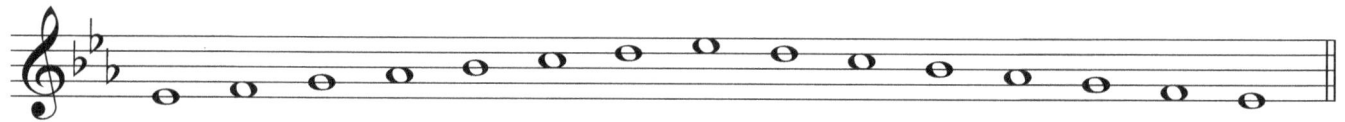

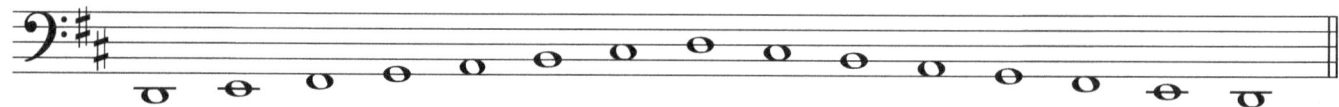

Page 33, No. 10

(a) half steps
(b) whole step
(c) accidental
(d) sharp
(e) flat
(f) natural
(g) enharmonic
(h) chromatic
(i) diatonic
(j) scale
(k) major scale
(l) WWHWWWH
(m) tonic
(n) key signature
(o) subdominant
(p) dominant

Page 34, No. 1 Review Two

Page 34, No. 2

Page 34, No. 3

Page 34, No. 4

Page 34, No. 5

Basic

Page 35, No. 6

(a) B♭ major (b) F♯, C♯
(c) C (d) B♭, E♭, A♭
(e) WWHWWWH (f) E
(g) E major (h) B♭, E♭, A, D♭
(i) F (j) C major
(k) sharp (l) flat
(m) F♭, C♭ (n) E♯, B♯
(o) natural

Page 35, No. 7

adagio	a slow tempo between andante and largo
allegro	fast
andante	moderately slow; at a walking pace
presto	very fast
moderato	at a moderate tempo

Page 36, No. 8

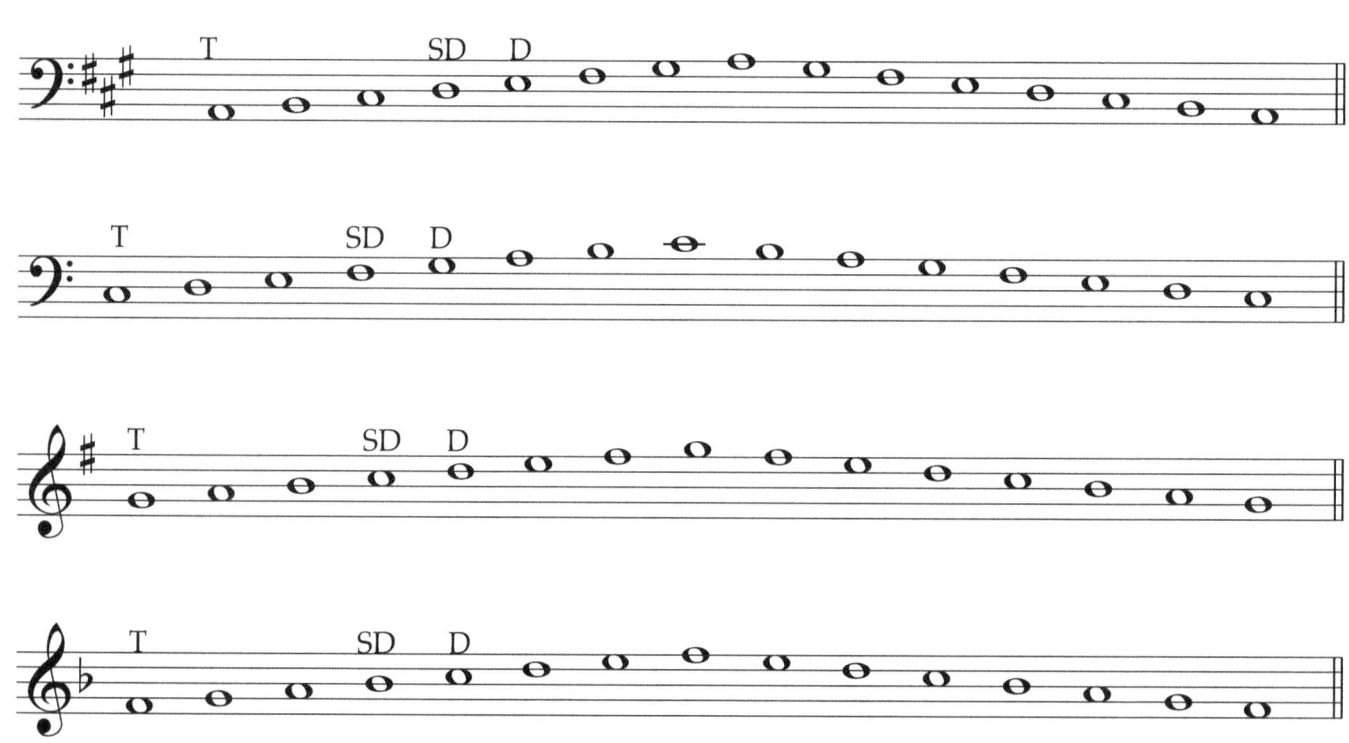

Page 36, No. 9

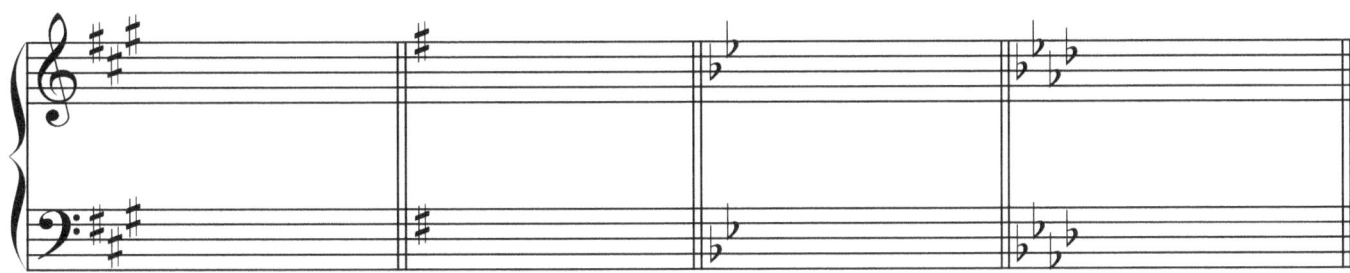

Page 37, No. 10

p, d, b, n, q, s, i, r, m, j, a, k, o, l, e, h, g, c, f

Page 38, No. 1

5   2   8   1   3   5   7   2   4   6

Page 38, No. 2

8   2   3   5   6   7   4   1   7   3

Page 38, No. 3

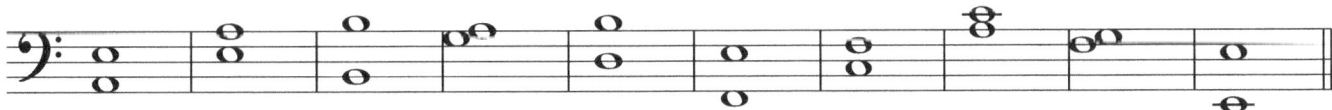

Page 39, No. 4

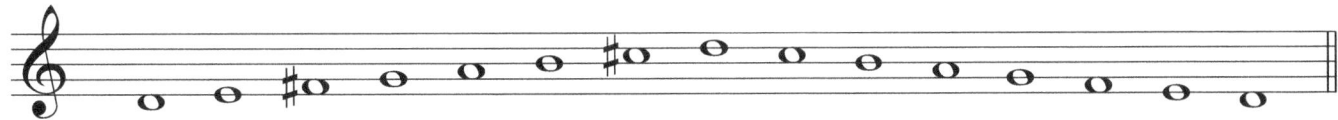

Page 39 No. 5

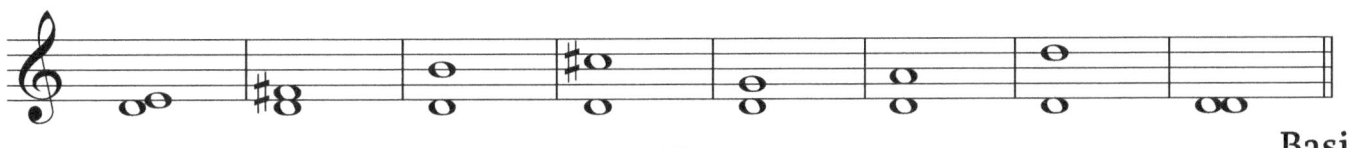

Basic

Page 39, No. 6

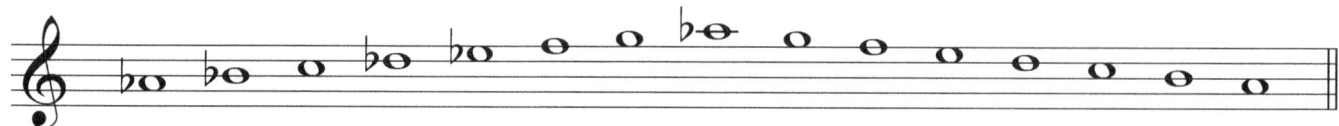

Page 39, No. 7

Page 40, No. 8

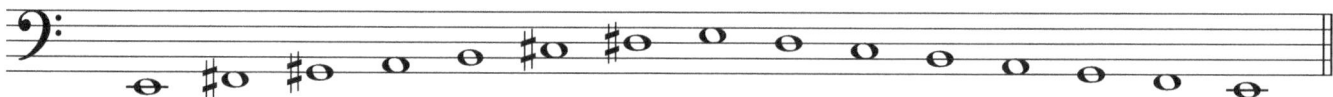

Page 40, No. 9

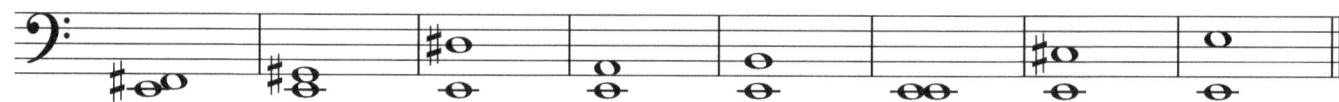

Page 41, No. 1

Basic

Page 41, No. 2

per 8	per 5	min 3	maj 3	per 5	min 7	per 4	per 8
maj 6	maj 7	maj 2	min 3	maj 3	per 5	per 4	maj 7
maj 6	min 2	maj 3	per 4	per 8	per 5	maj 7	min 3

Page 42, No. 3

maj 3	per 5	per 4	maj 2	per 8	min 3	per 4	min 7
min 7	min 6	maj 3	min 6	maj 2	maj 3	per 5	maj 3
per 8	maj 7	min 7	maj 2	maj 6	per 8	min 7	maj 6

Page 42, No. 4

per 4   maj 7   min 7   per 5   maj 2   min 6   maj 3   maj 6

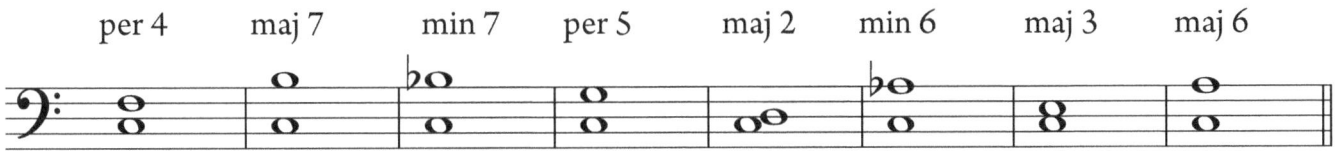

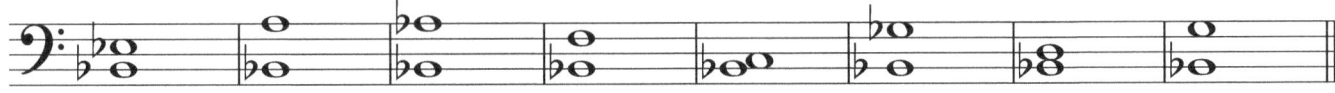

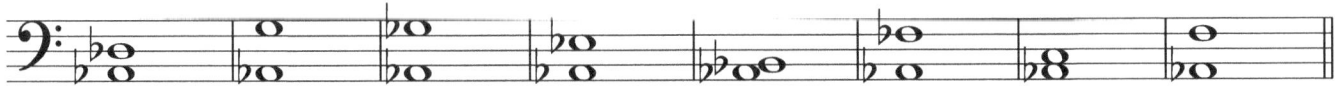

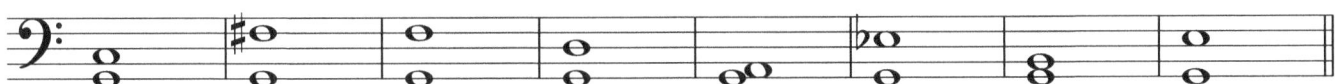

Basic

Page 43, No. 5

min 3	per 5	per 8	min 6	per 4	per 5	min 3	per 5
per 4	maj 6	maj 6	per 5	maj 2	maj 3	min 3	per 4
min 6	maj 7	per 8	per 5	maj 3	min 3	min 2	maj 7

Page 43, No. 6

per 4   per 4   per 5   min 2   per 4   min 2   maj 2

per 4   maj 3   min 3   per 5   per 4   maj 3   min 3   min 3   maj 2

maj 2   maj 2   min 3   maj 2   min 3   maj 6   maj 2   maj 2   maj 2   maj 3   per 5

Page 45, No. 1

B minor	D minor	E minor
F# minor	C# minor	G minor
C minor	F minor	A minor

Page 45, No. 2

A♭ major	B♭ major	F major	E♭ major
F minor	G minor	D minor	C minor
E♭ major	E major	G major	A major
C minor	C# minor	E minor	F# minor

Page 45, No. 3

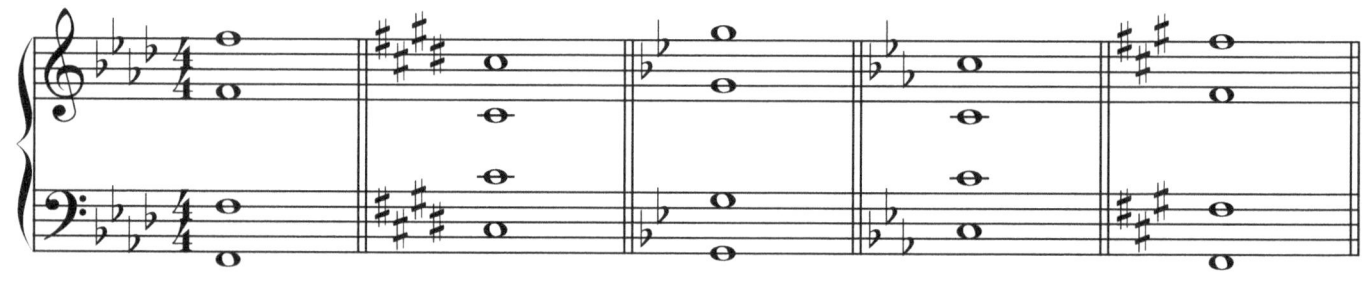

Page 46, No. 1

Basic

Page 47, No. 1

F harmonic minor

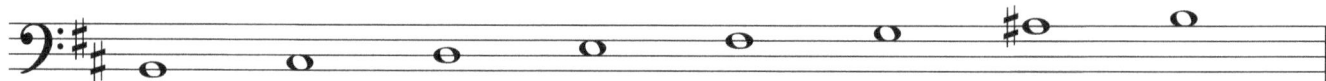

B harmonic minor

F# harmonic minor

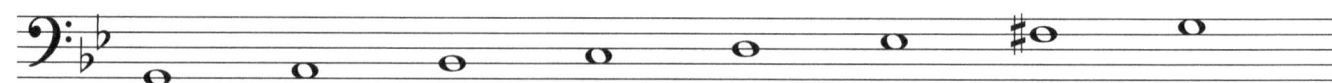

G harmonic minor

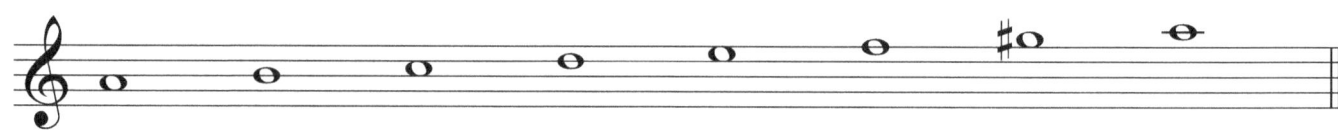

A harmonic minor

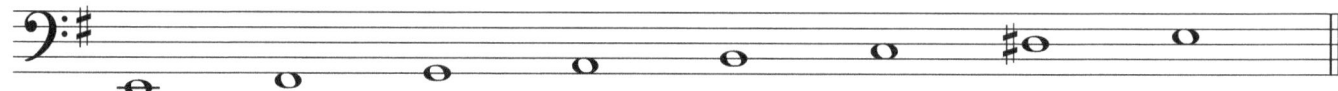

E harmonic minor

Page 48, No. 2

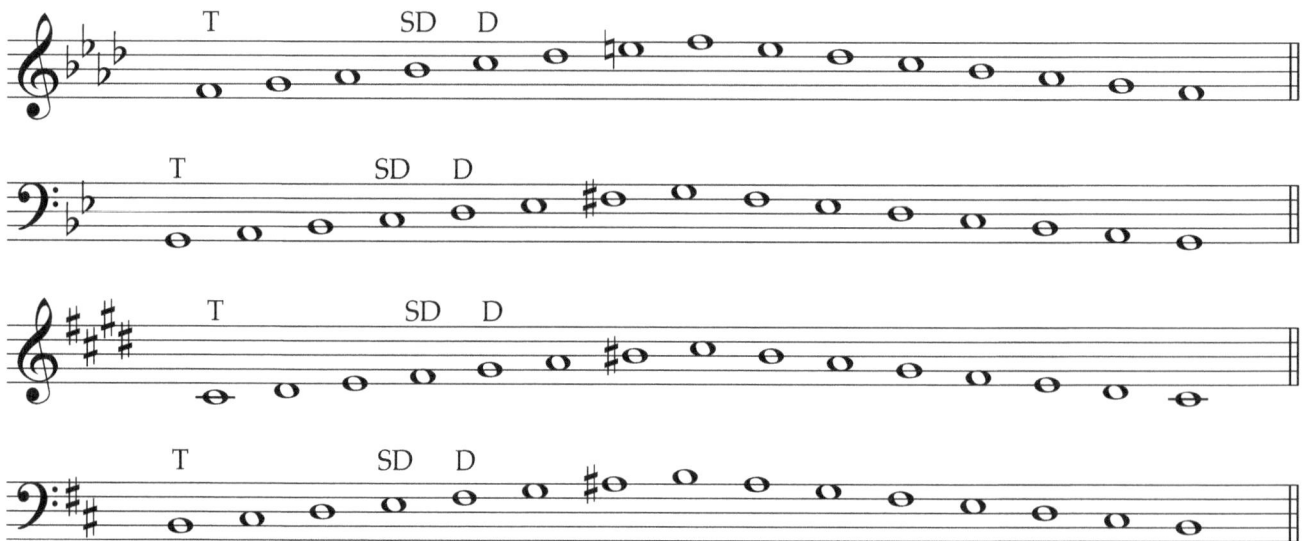

Page 49, No. 1

B melodic minor

C♯ melodic minor

G melodic minor

C melodic minor

Page 50, No. 2

Basic

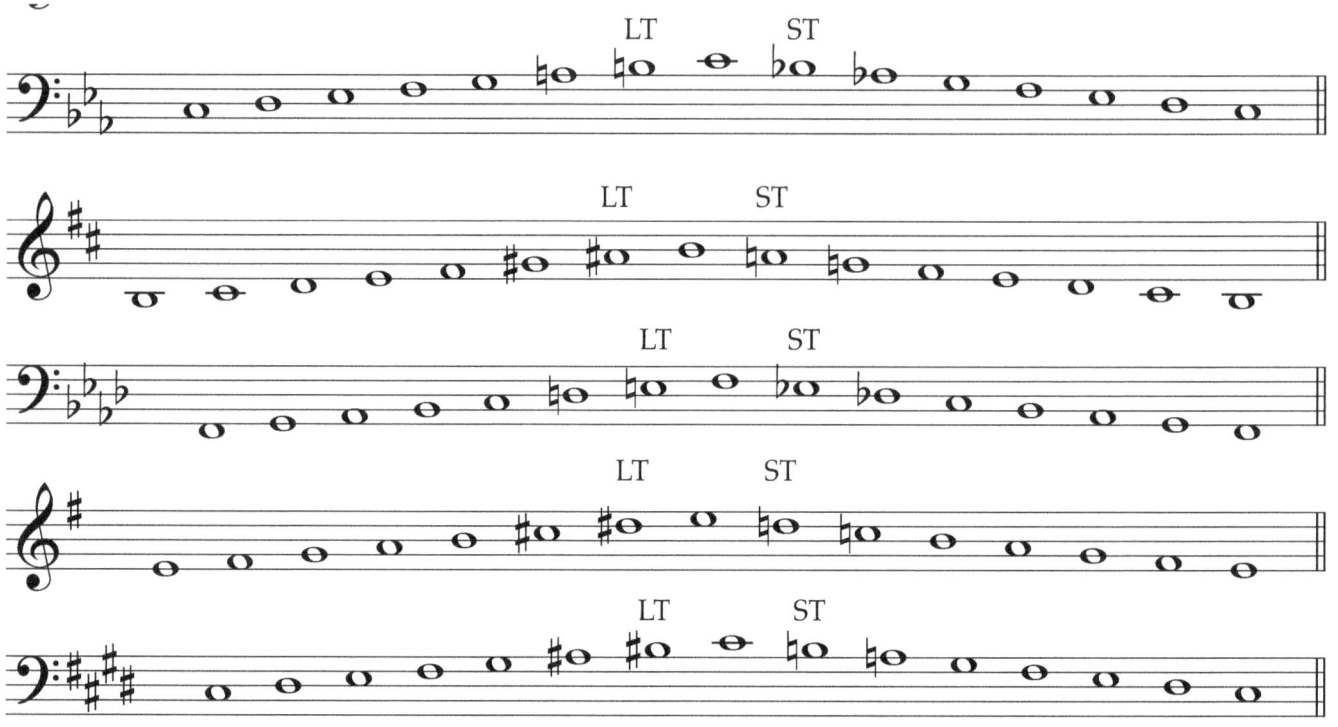

Page 51, No. 3

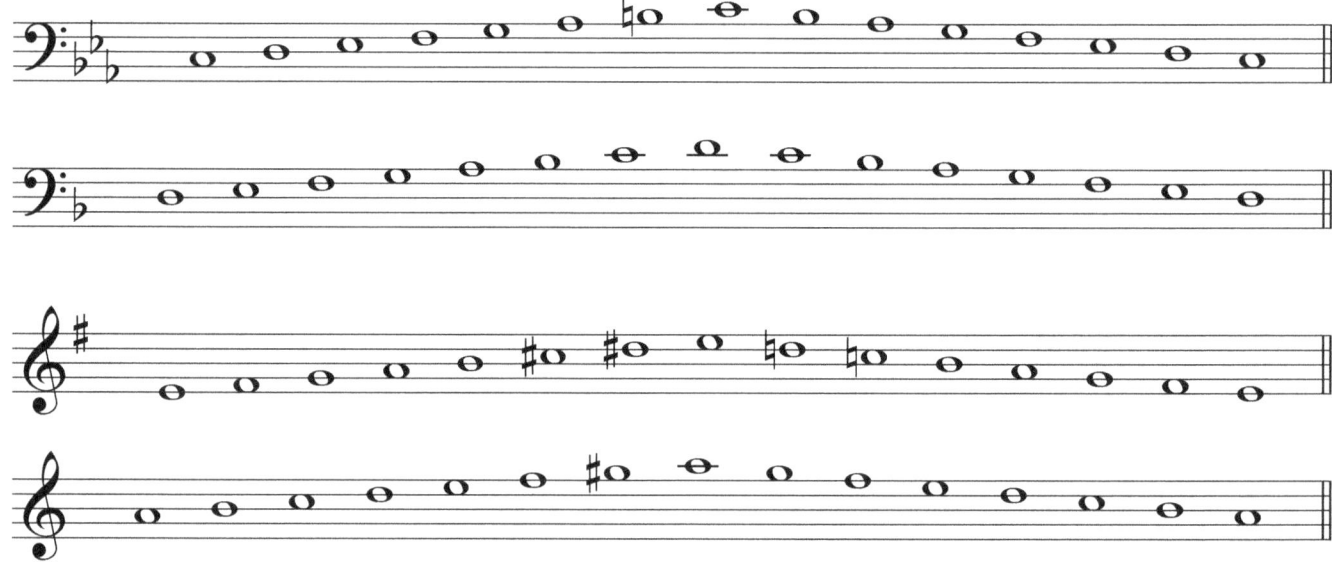

24

Basic

Page 52, No. 5

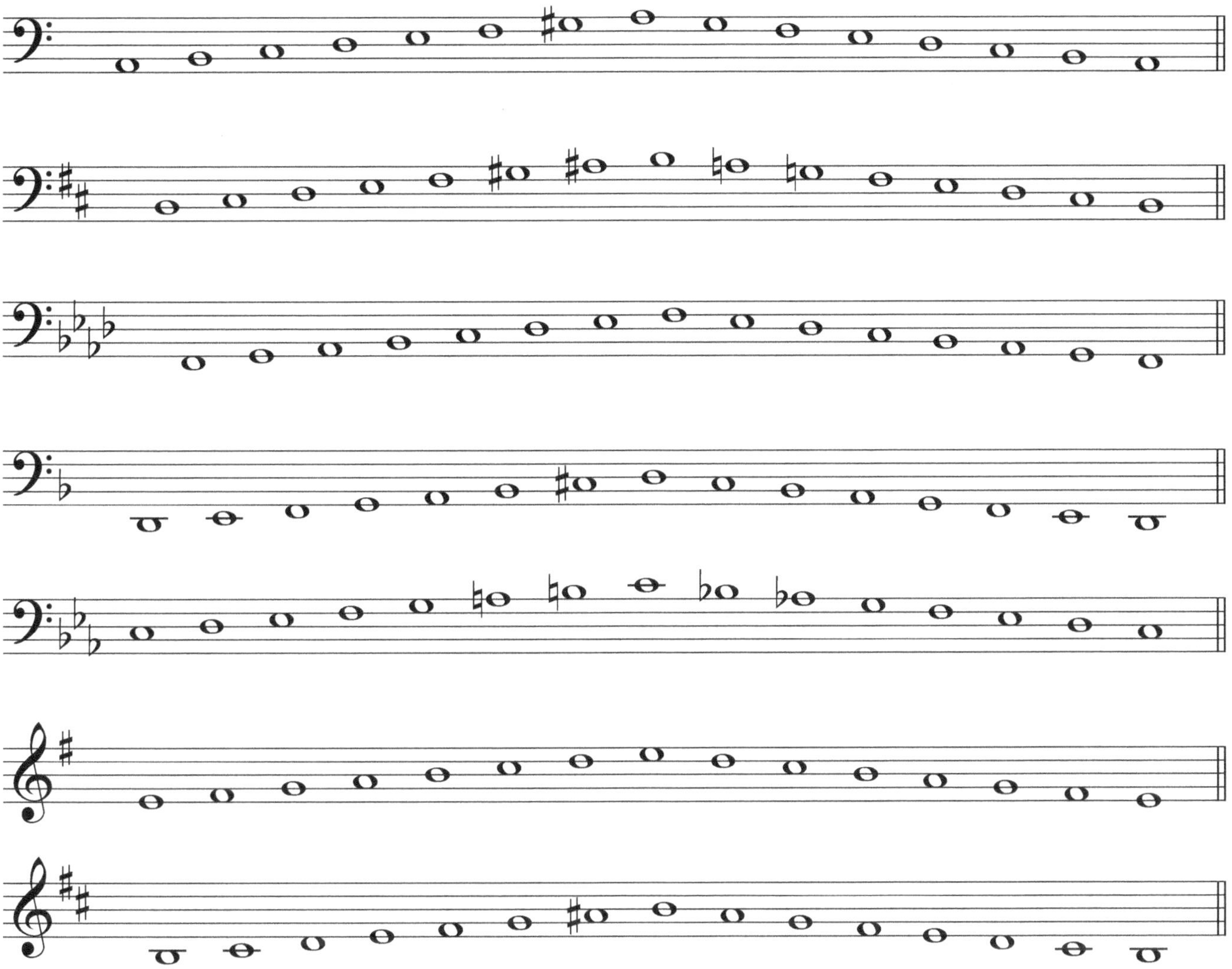

Page 53, No. 1 Review Three

min 6   maj 3   per 8   min 3   per 4   per 5   maj 2   maj 7   maj 3   maj 6

per 5   min 3   maj 7   maj 2   per 4   maj 6   min 6   per 8   maj 6   maj 3

Page 53, No. 2

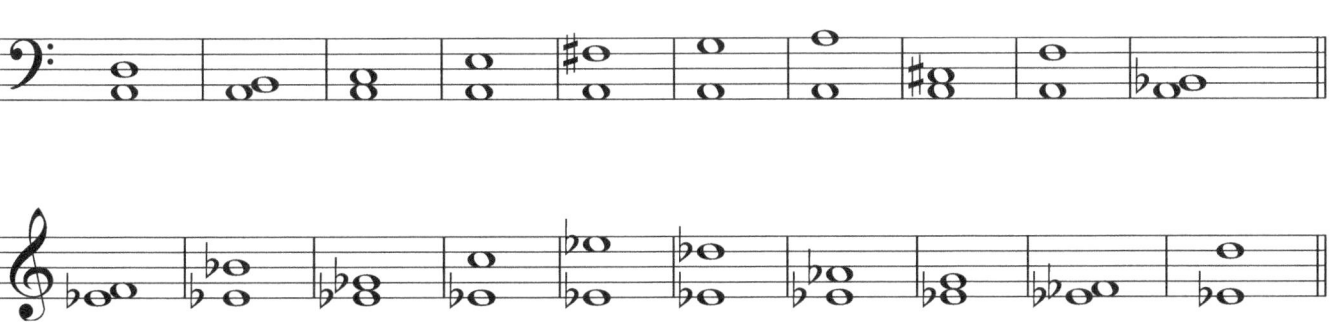

25

Basic

Page 53, No. 3

E minor	C# minor
B minor	A minor
F# minor	G minor
D minor	C minor
F minor	

Page 54, No. 4

B♭, E♭, A♭
B minor
C#
A♭ major
C
F#, C#, G#, D#
F# minor
F#
F major
F#
A

Page 54 and 55, No. 5

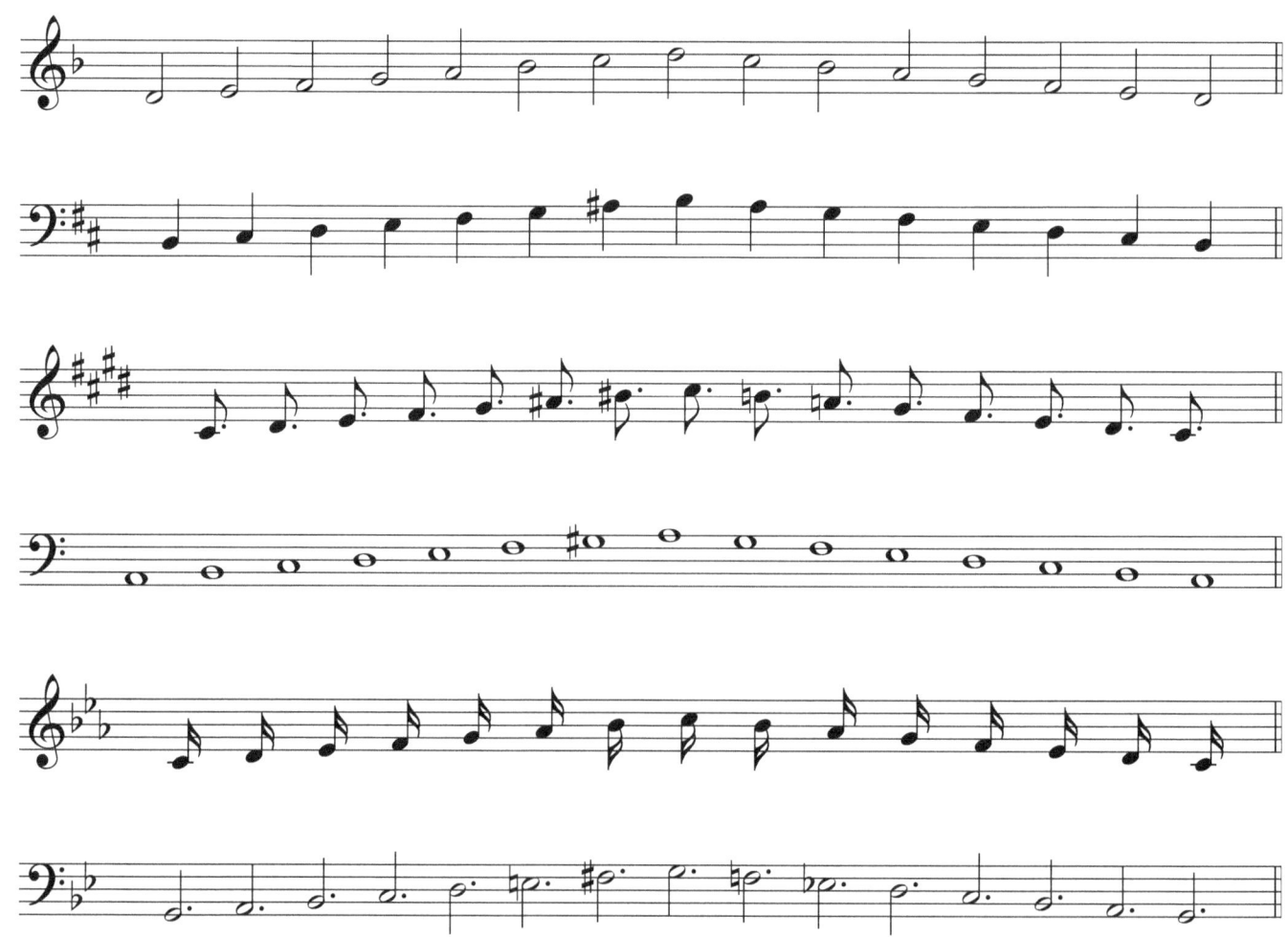

Page 55, No. 6

Page 58, No. 1

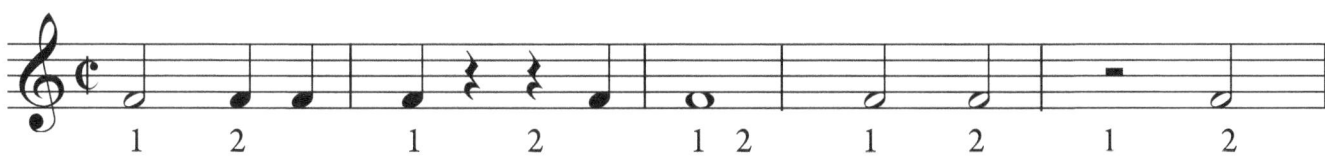

Basic

Page 60, No. 2

Page 62, No. 3

Page 64, No. 4

4/4   2/4   3/2   2/2   3/4   4/4   2/2

Basic

Page 65, No. 5

Georg Philipp Telemann
(1681-1767)

Giacomo Puccini
(1858-1924)

Franz Schubert
(1797-1828)

Geroge Frideric Handel
(1685-1759)

Franz Schubert
(1797-1828)

Traditional

Giacomo Puccini
(1858-1924)

Basic

Page 66, No. 6

3/8   4/4   4/4   3/4   4/4   3/4   4/4

Page 69, No. 1 (other options are possible)

Page 70, No. 2

4/4   3/4   3/8   4/2   2/4   2/8   2/2   4/4   2/8   3/8

Basic

Page 71, No. 3 (other options are possible)

Page 73, No. 1

fifth:	C	D	E	A	G	F#
third:	A	B♭	C#	F	E♭	D
root:	F	G	A	D	C	B

Page 73, No. 2

major major major major minor major
minor major major major minor minor

Basic

Page 73, No. 3

Page 73, No. 4

Page 74, No. 5

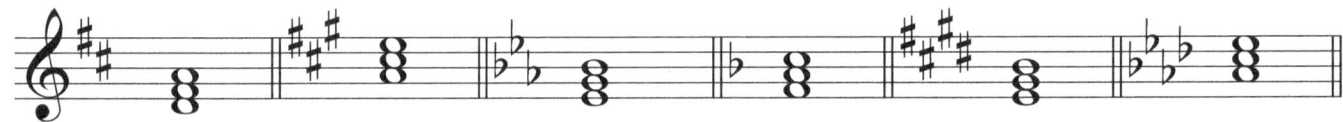

Page 74, No. 6

Page 74, No. 7

Page 74, No. 8

Page 74, No. 9

Page 74, No. 10

Basic

Page 75, No. 11

key:	D major	C minor	F major	G minor	C major
degree:	IV	V	I	V	IV

key:	A minor	B♭ major	G major	A major	D minor
degree:	I	V	IV	I	V

Page 75, No. 12

Page 76, No. 1 Review Four (other options are possible)

Page 76, No. 2

Page 76, No. 3

4/2   3/8   3/4

Basic

Page 77, No. 4

Page 77, No. 5

key:	G major	F major	D major	G minor
degree:	tonic	dominant	tonic	dominant

key:	B♭ major	E♭ major	C♯ minor	F minor
degree:	tonic	dominant	dominant	tonic

key:	A♭ major	E minor	G minor	A major
degree:	tonic	subdominant	tonic	tonic

Page 77, No. 6

rallentando	slowing down
a tempo	return to the previous tempo
forte	loud
pianissimo	very soft
mezzo piano	moderately soft
Tempo I, Tempo primo	return to the original speed or tempo
fortissimo	very loud
mezzo forte	moderately loud

Page 79, No. 1

G major
D minor
G minor
A minor
B minor
F major
A major
E flat major

Basic

Page 81, No. 1

D minor

Page 81, No. 2

E major

Page 81, No. 3

E♭ major

Page 81, No. 4

F# minor

Page 82, No. 5

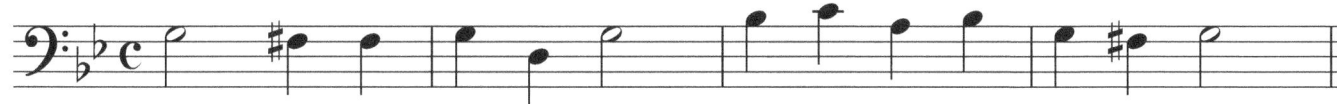

G minor

Page 82, No. 6

A major

Page 82, No. 7

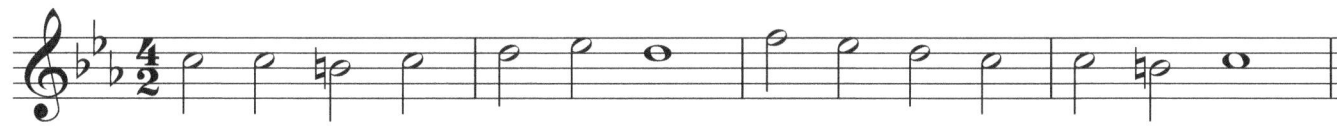

C minor

Basic

Page 82, No. 8

G major

Page 83, No. 1 Review Five

D major

Page 83, No. 2

F major

Page 83, No. 3

C minor

Page 84, No. 4

C minor

Page 84, No. 5

A major

Page 84, No. 6

forte
crescendo
ritardando
dolce
pianissimo

Page 85, No. 1

Study in C

(a) What is the title of this excerpt? **Study in C**

(b) Name the composer of this excerpt: **Carl Czerny**

(c) Add the time signature to the excerpt. **4/4**

(d) Define the term at A: **Allegro - play fast**

(e) Explain the sign at B: **piano - play soft**

(f) Explain the sign at C: **forte - play loud**

(g) Name the intervals at D: **min 7**   E: **maj 3**

(h) Name the triad at F: **G major**

(i) Name the sign at G: **half rest**

(j) Name the highest note: **G**   Name the lowest note: **C**

Basic

Page 86, No. 2

(a) Give the title of this excerpt: **Carefree**

(b) Name the composer of this excerpt: **Daniel Gottlob Turk**

(c) Add the time signature to the excerpt. **4/4**

(d) How many measures are there in this excerpt? **8**

(e) Define the word at A: **at a moderate tempo**

(f) Explain the sign at B: **mezzo piano - play moderately soft**

(g) Explain the sign at C: **quarter rest - silence for one beat**

(h) Name the intervals at D: **maj 3** E: **maj 2** F: **per 8**

Basic

Page 87, No. 3

Waltz

Carl Czerny
(1791-1857)

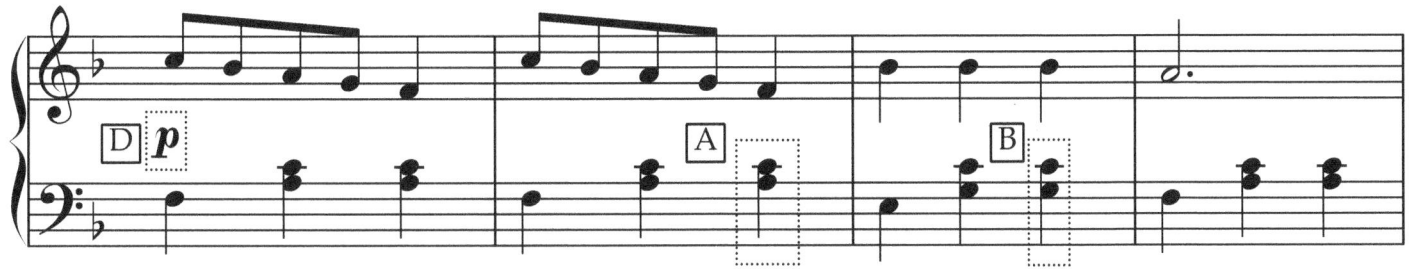

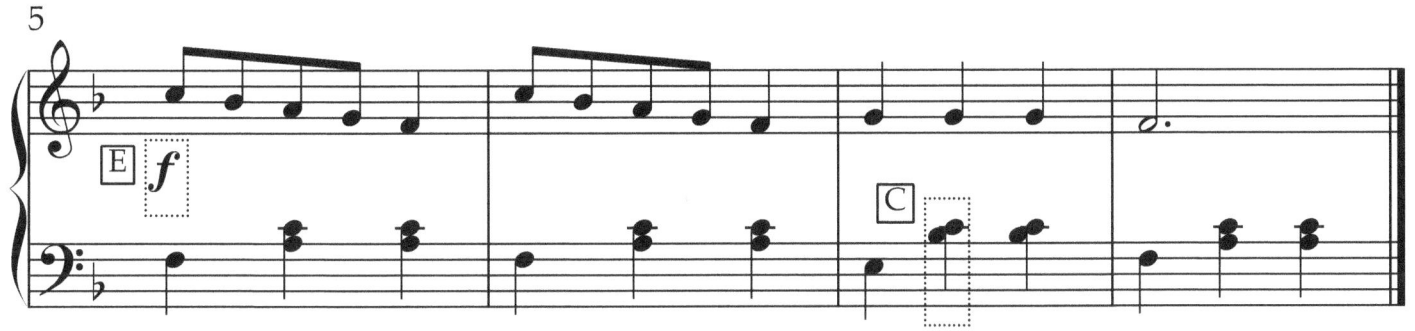

(a) Add the time signature to the music. **3/4**

(b) Give the title of this excerpt: **Waltz**

(c) Name the composer of this excerpt: **Carl Czerny**

(d) Name the key of this excerpt: **F major**

(e) How many measures are there in this excerpt? **8**

(f) Name the intervals at A: **min 3** B: **per 4** C: **maj 2**

(g) Explain the sign at D: **piano - play soft**

(h) Explain the sign at E: **forte - play loud**

Basic

Page 88, No. 4

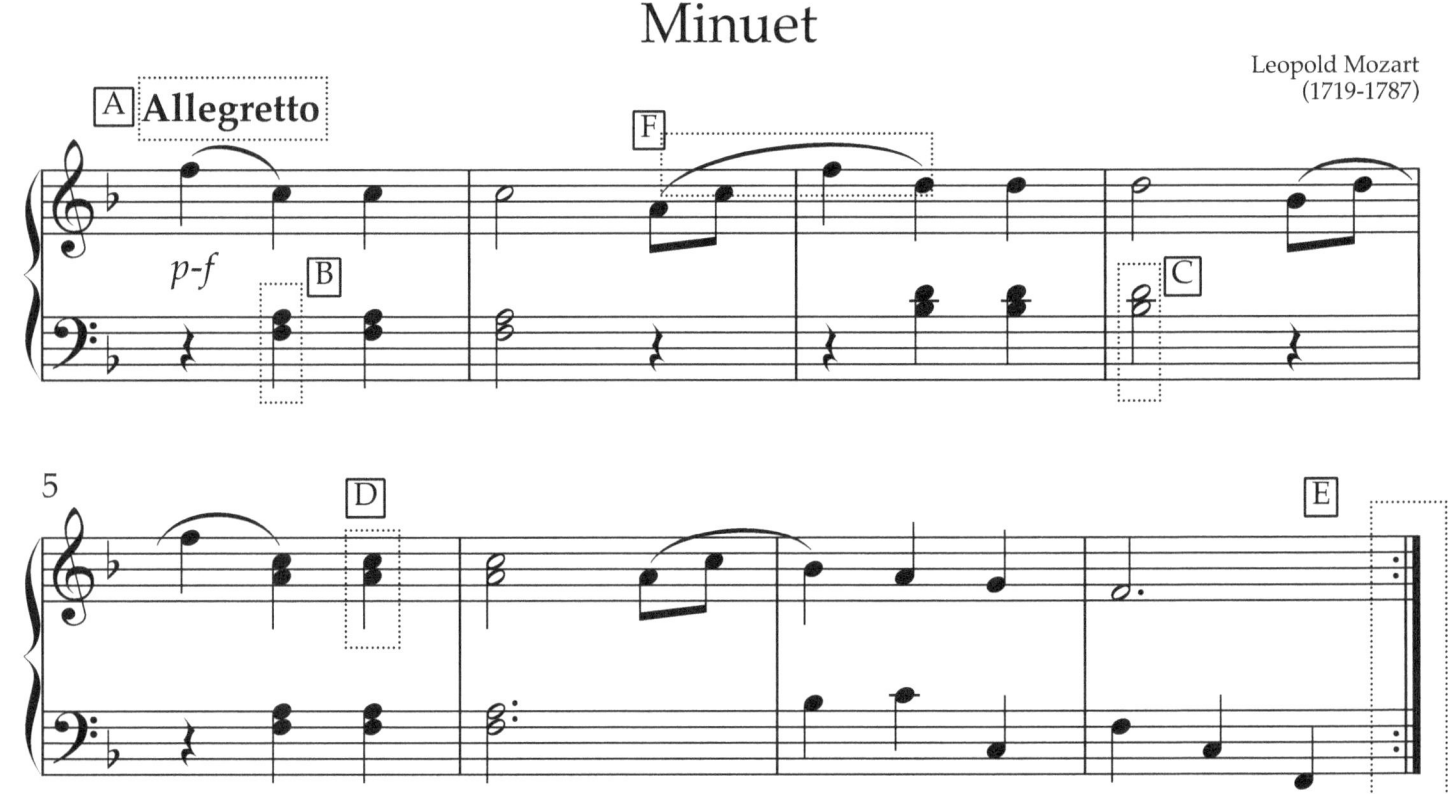

(a) Name the composer of this excerpt: **Leopold Mozart**

(b) Write the title of this excerpt: **Minuet**

(c) How many measures are there in this excerpt? **8 or 16 with repeat**

(d) Add the time signature to the music. **3/4**

(e) Define the term at A: **fairly fast (a little slower than allegro)**

(f) Name the intervals at B, C, and D: **maj 3   maj 3   min 3**

(g) Explain the sign at E: **Repeat sign - repeat from the beginning**

(h) Explain the curved line at F: **slur - play notes smoothly connected**

(i) Name the highest note: **F**   Name the lowest note: **F**

Basic

Practice Test

Page 89, No. 1

B A C F♯ A D C D A♭ G

Page 89, No. 2 (other options are possible)

Page 89, No. 3

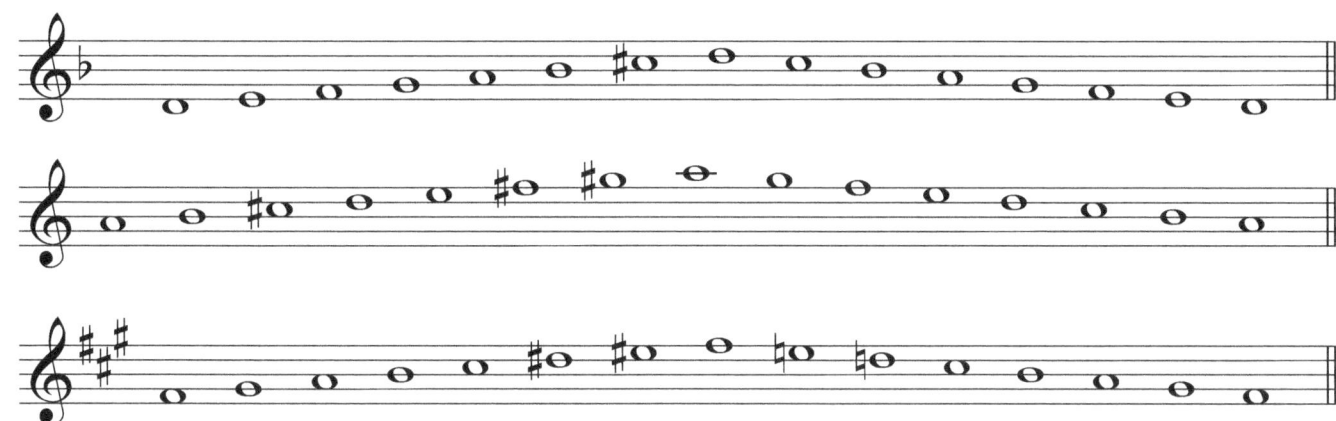

Page 89, No. 4

min 3   min 7   per 4   per 5   maj 6

Page 89, No. 5

W C D C D D W W D C

Page 90, No. 6

2/4   3/8
4/4   3/4

Page 90, No. 7

Basic

Page 90, No. 8

Page 90, No. 9

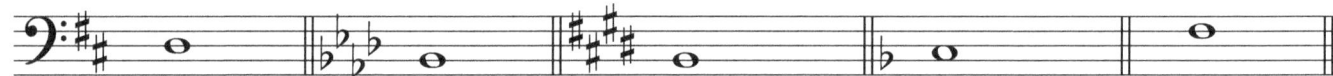

Page 90, No. 10

A minor

Page 91, No. 11

(a) Add the correct time signature directly on the music. 3/4

(b) Name of the composer of this excerpt. Wolfgang Amadeus Mozart

(c) When did the composer live? 1756-1791

(d) Name the highest note in this excerpt. A

(e) Name the intervals at A:min 3 B: min 3

(f) Name the sign at the C: tie

(g) How many measures are in this excerpt? 8 or 16 with the repeat

(h) How many accidentals are in this excerpt? 6

(i) Define *allegretto*: Fairly fast, but not as fast as allegro

History Answers

Page 98

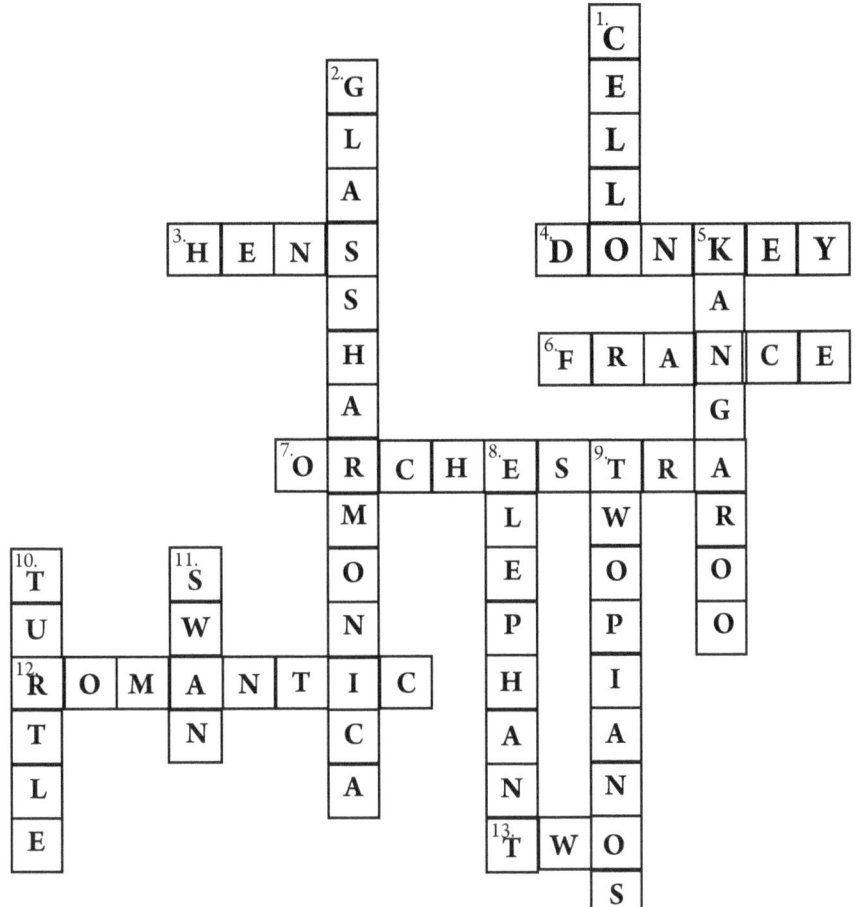

Page 99

a. ☑Conductor
b. ☑Maracas
c. ☑French Horn
d. ☑France
e. ☑3
f. ☑2 pianos
g. ☑Wolf
h. ☑Glass Harmonic
i. ☑Cello
j. ☑Program Music

Basic

Page 102

1. Where was Prokofiev born? **Russia**
2. At what age did Prokofiev begin composing? **five**
3. In what musical era did he compose? **Modern**
4. Peter and the Wolf is written for narrator and **orchestra**
5. What type of music is Peter and the Wolf? **Program**
6. Name 4 animals in Peter and the Wolf. **Wolf, duck, cat, bird**
7. What instruments are used to portray Peter? **strings**
8. What instrument is used to portray the grandfather? **bassooon**
9. What instument is used to portray the duck? **oboe**

Page 105

a. Austria
b. His father
c. classical
d. french horn
e. movements
f. rondo
g. piano
h. 12
i. theme
j. Twinkle Twinkle, Baa Baa Black Sheep, Alphabet Song

Page 111

a) Baroque
b) 1600 -1750
c) Germany
d) A book of Baroque keyboard pieces
e) Carl Phillip Emmanuel Bach, Johann Christian Bach
f) Dances, Arias, Chorales, Minuet, Gavotte, Gigue
g) Harpsichord
h) Keyboard
i) France
j) 3/4
k) France
l) Yes
m) Allegro, Presto
n) three
o) At the end

Basic

Page 114

a. Who composed Young Persons Guide to the Orchestra? **Benjamin Britten**

b. In what country was he born? **England or Great Britain**

c. In what era did he live? **Modern**

d. Who composed the theme on which this work is based? **Henry Purcell**

e. What era did this composer live? **Baroque**

f. How many variations are in Young Persons Guide to the Orchestra? **13**

g. What are the four instrument families featured in this composition?

    1. **Strings**
    2. **Woodwinds**
    3. **Brass**
    4. **Percussion**

h. What type of piece is the final movement of this composition? **Fugue**

Page 118

a. Who composed *The Nutcracker*? **Piotr Ilyich Tchaikovsky**

b. In what country was he born? **Russia**

c. In what era did he live? **Romantic**

d. How many symphonies did he write? **Six**

e. What type of work is *The Nutcracker*? **Ballet**

f. Name a dance from *The Nutcracker*. **Waltz of the flowers, Dance of the Sugar Plum Fairy**

g. Who choreographed *The Nutcracker*?

    1. **Marius Petipa**
    2. **Lev Ivanov**

h. What is a choreographer? **A choreographer designs the dances for a ballet.**

i. What unique instrument is featured in *The Nutcracker*? **Celesta**

Basic

Elementary Music Rudiments Intermediate Answers

Page 9, No. 1

Page 10, No. 2

Page 10, No. 3

Page 10, No. 4

Page 10, No. 5

Page 10, No. 6

Page 12, No. 1

key:	C major	G major	D major	A major
sharps:	none	F#	F#, C#	F#, C#, G#

key:	E major	B major	F# major	C# major
sharps:	F#, C#, G#, D#	F#, C#, G#, D#, A#	F#, C#, G#, D#, A#, E#	F#, C#, G#, D#, A#, E#, B#

Page 13, No. 2

key:	C major	F major	B♭ major	E♭ major
sharps:	none	B♭	B♭, E♭	B♭, E♭, A♭

key:	A♭ major	D♭ major	G♭ major	C♭ major
sharps:	B♭, E♭, A♭, D♭	B♭, E♭, A♭, D♭, G♭	B♭, E♭, A♭, D♭, G♭, C♭	B♭, E♭, A♭, D♭, G♭, C♭, F♭

Page 13, No. 3 (other options are possible)

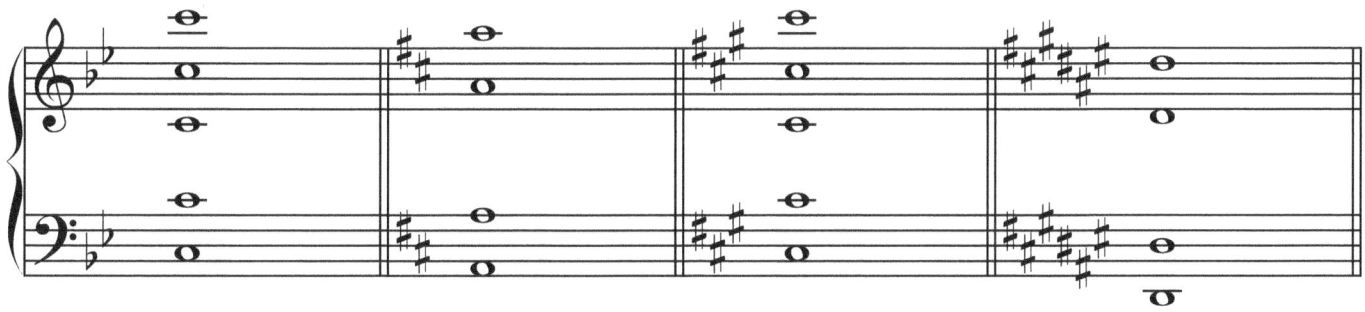

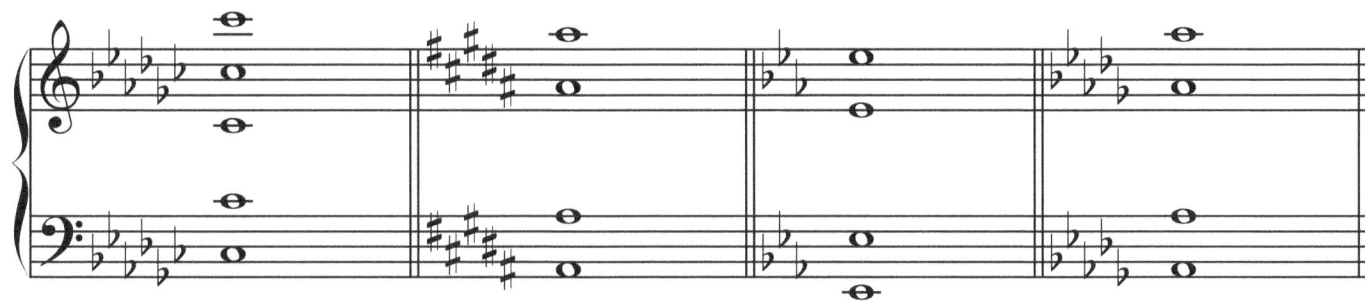

Page 14, No. 1

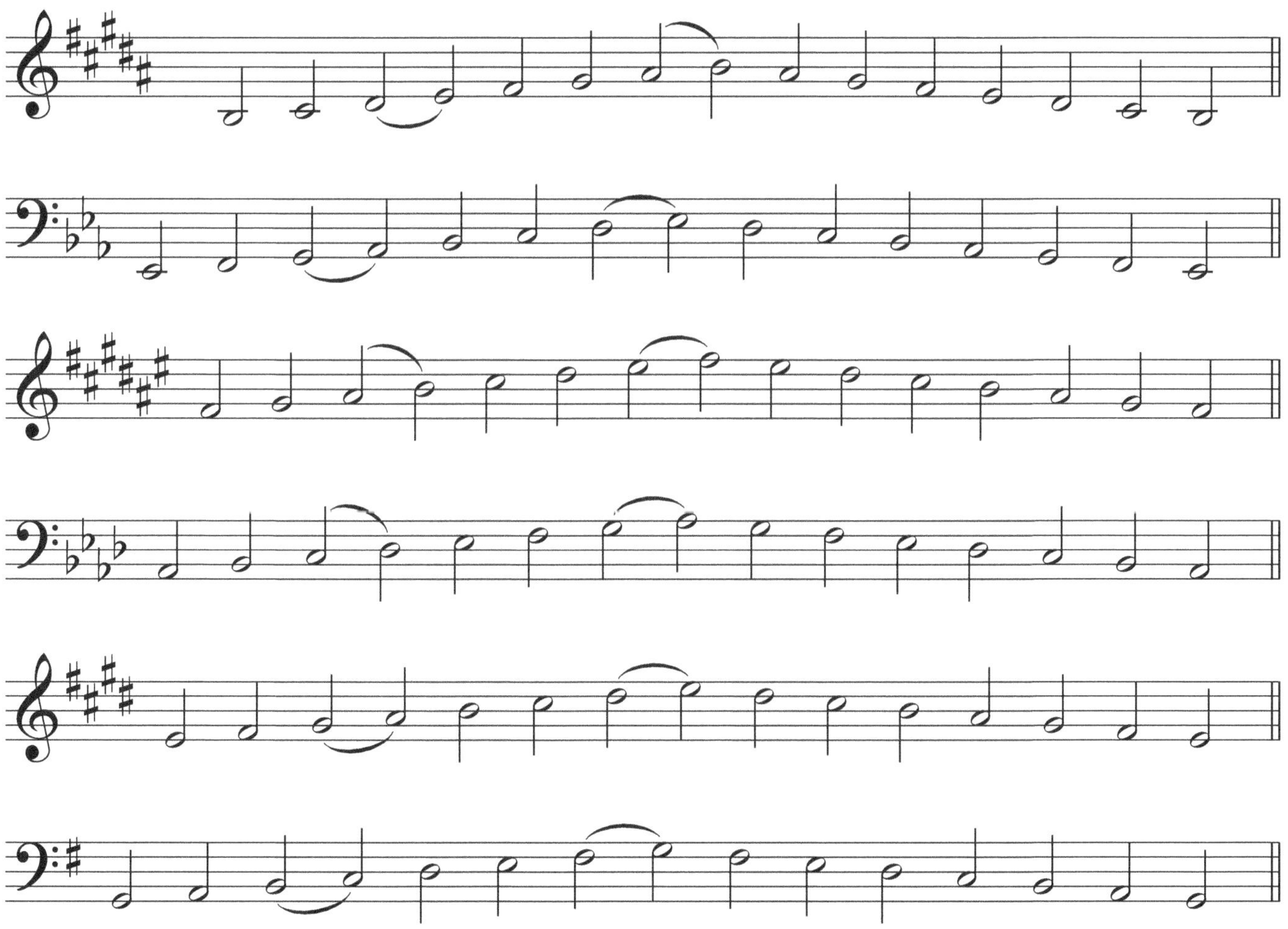

Intermediate

Page 15, No. 2

Page 16, No. 3

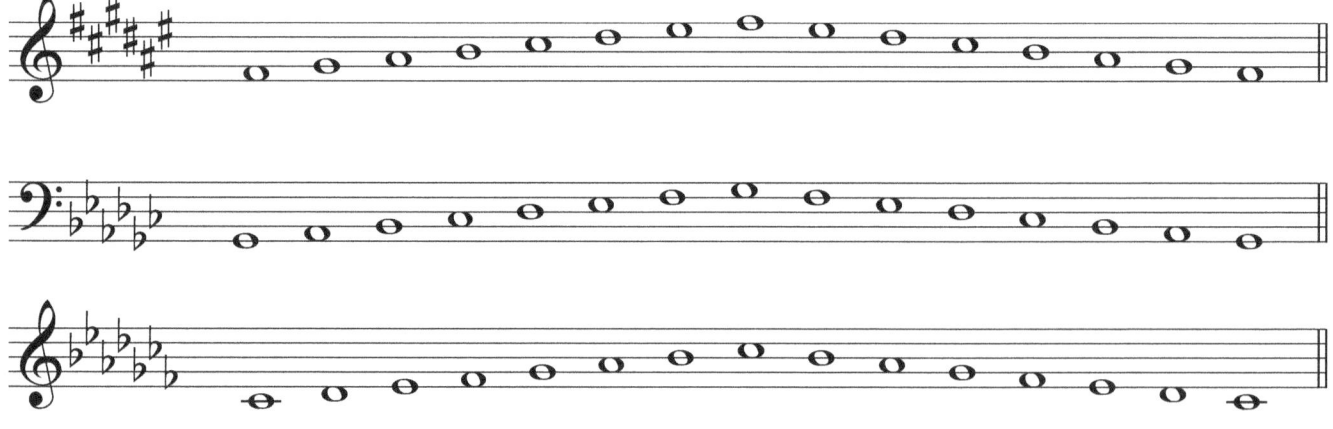

Intermediate

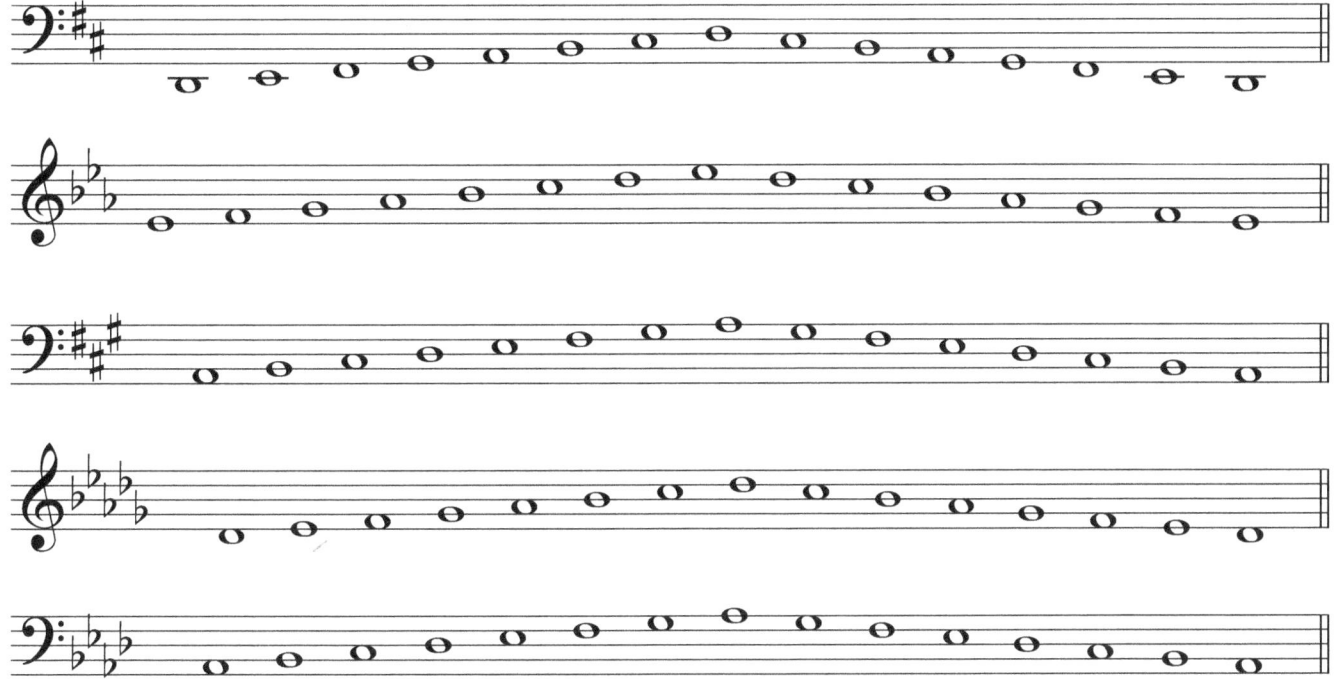

Page 17, No. 4

G major $\hat{5}$ dominant	B♭ major $\hat{2}$ supertonic	D♭ major $\hat{2}$ supertonic	F♯ major $\hat{1}$ tonic
E major $\hat{3}$ mediant	A♭ major $\hat{6}$ submediant	A major $\hat{4}$ subdominant	G♭ major $\hat{7}$ leading tone
G major $\hat{4}$ subdominant	F major $\hat{7}$ leading tone	E♭ major $\hat{3}$ mediant	E major $\hat{5}$ dominant
C major $\hat{7}$ leading tone	B major $\hat{2}$ supertonic	E♭ major $\hat{6}$ submediant	D major $\hat{1}$ tonic
C♯ major $\hat{1}$ tonic	D♭ major $\hat{6}$ submediant	G major $\hat{2}$ supertonic	G♭ major $\hat{3}$ mediant

Page 19, No. 1

C♯ harmonic minor
C melodic minor
E natural minor
G♯ melodic minor
E♭ harmonic minor

Intermediate

Page 20, No. 2

Page 21, No. 3

A minor	D minor	A# minor	G minor
D# minor	C minor	G# minor	F minor
C# minor	B♭ minor	F# minor	E♭ minor
B minor	A♭ minor	E minor	G minor
A# minor	B♭ minor	E minor	E♭ minor

Intermediate

Page 21, No. 4

D# minor	G minor
E minor	C minor
A# minor	C# minor
F minor	B♭ minor
A minor	D minor
G# minor	E♭ minor
F# minor	A♭ minor
B minor	

Page 22, No. 5

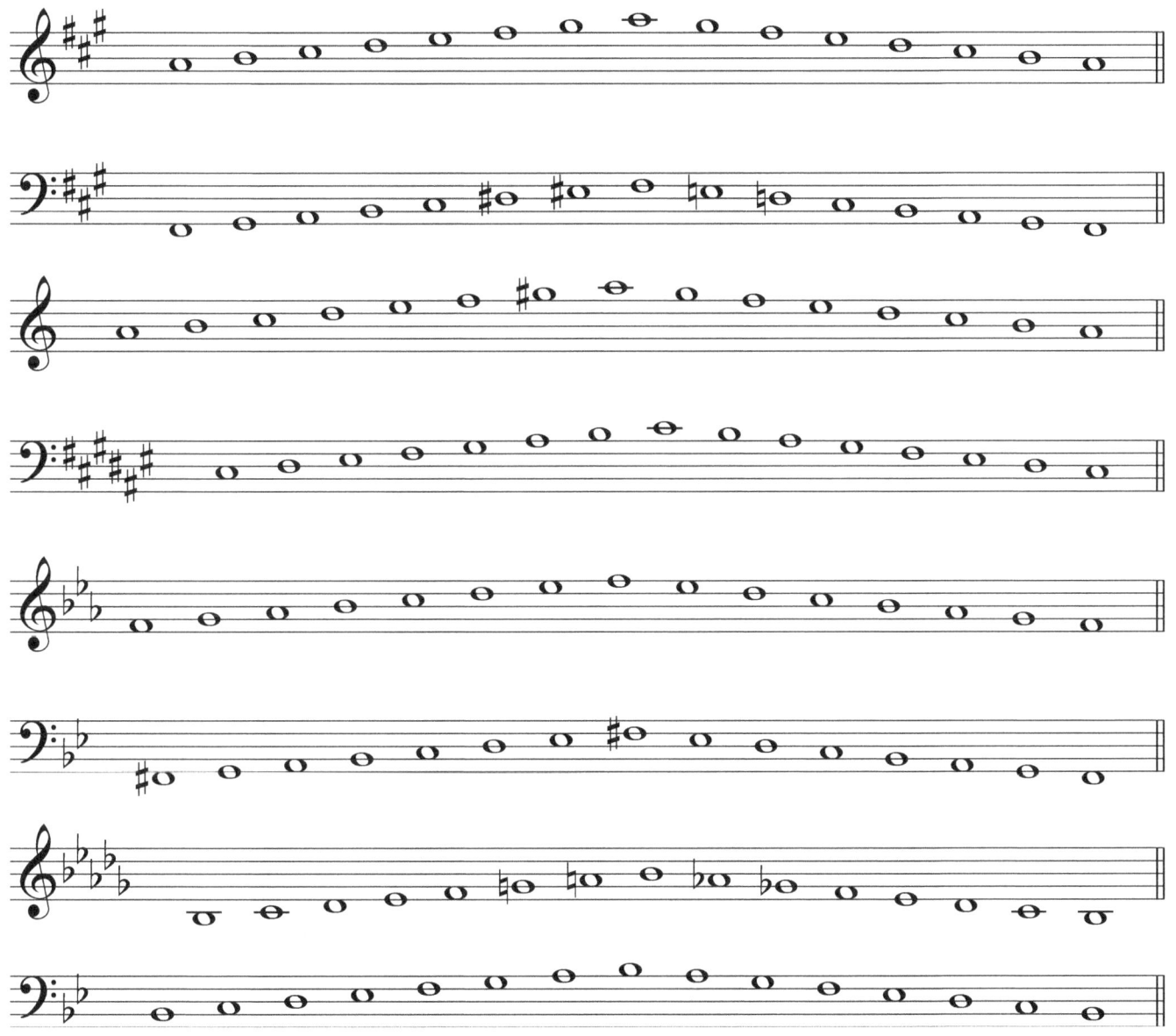

Intermediate

Page 23, No. 6

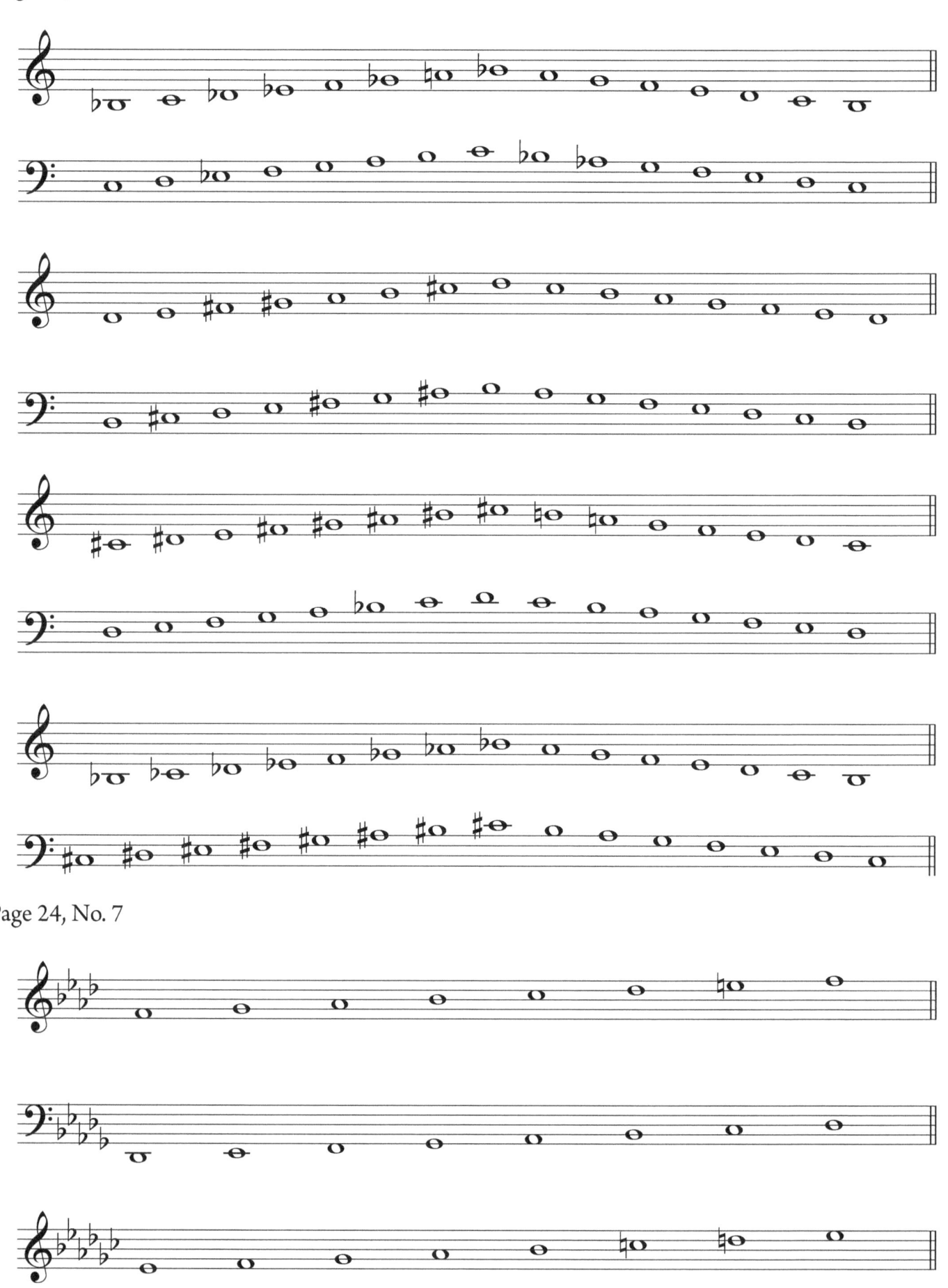

Page 24, No. 7

Intermediate

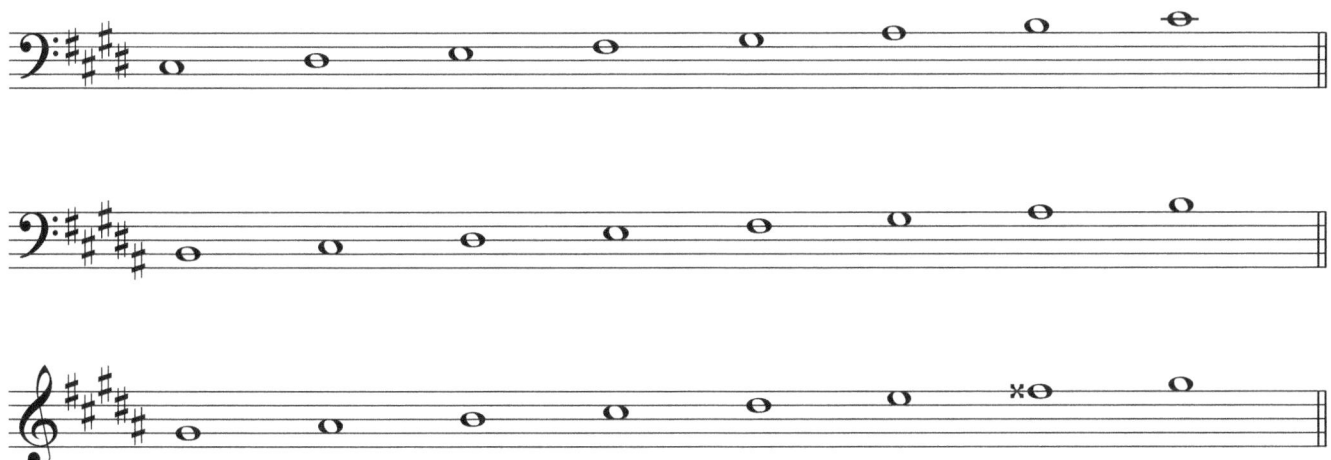

Page 26, No. 1

Intermediate

ok to use G
again on descent

Page 27, No. 2

Page 28, No. 3

Intermediate

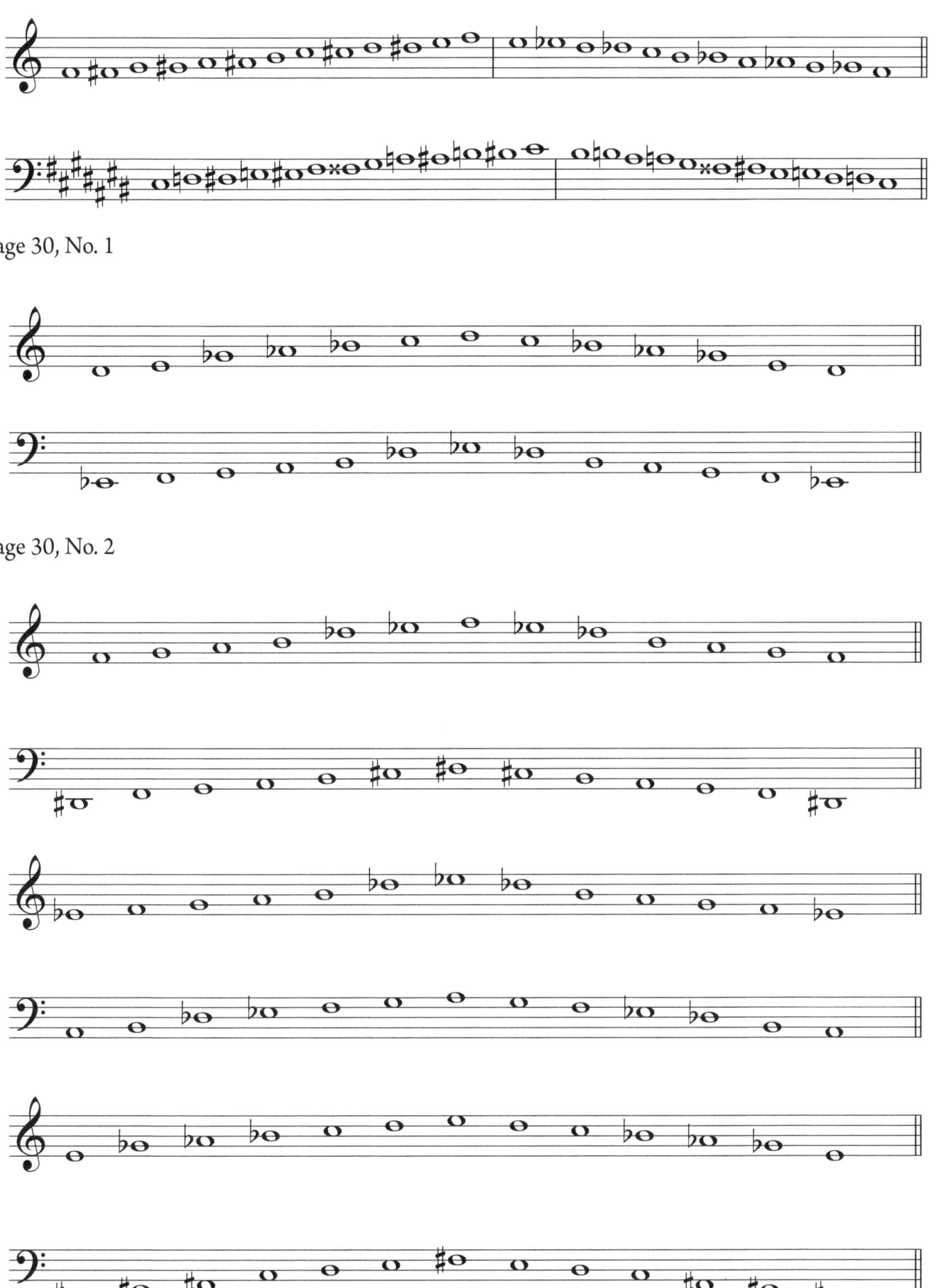

Page 30, No. 1

Page 30, No. 2

Intermediate

Page 31, No. 1

Page 33, No. 1

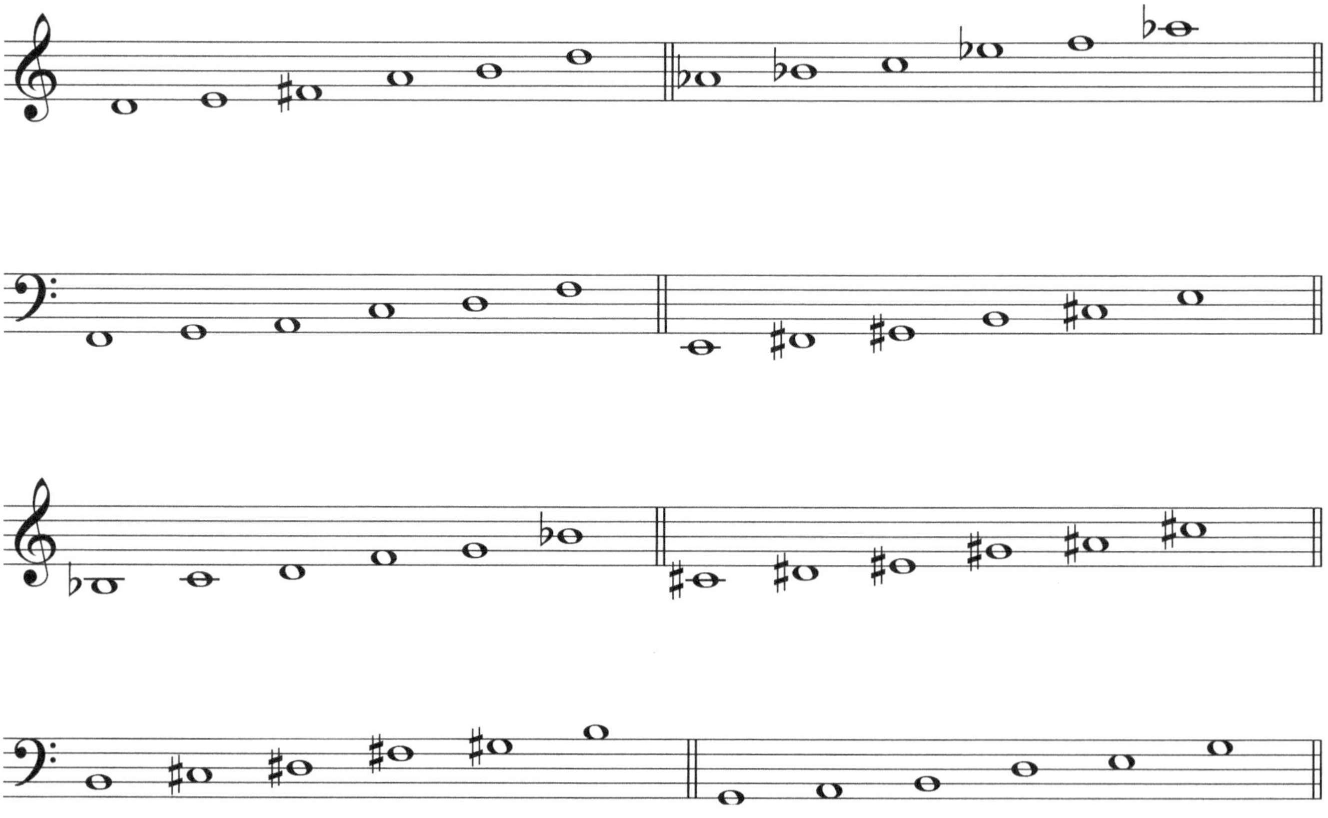

Intermediate

Page 34

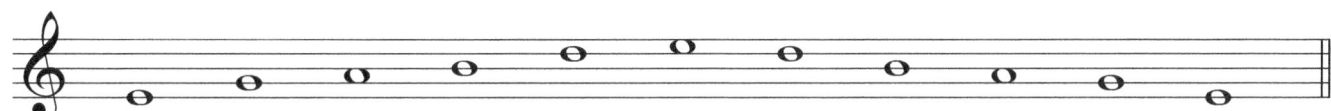

Page 35, No. 2

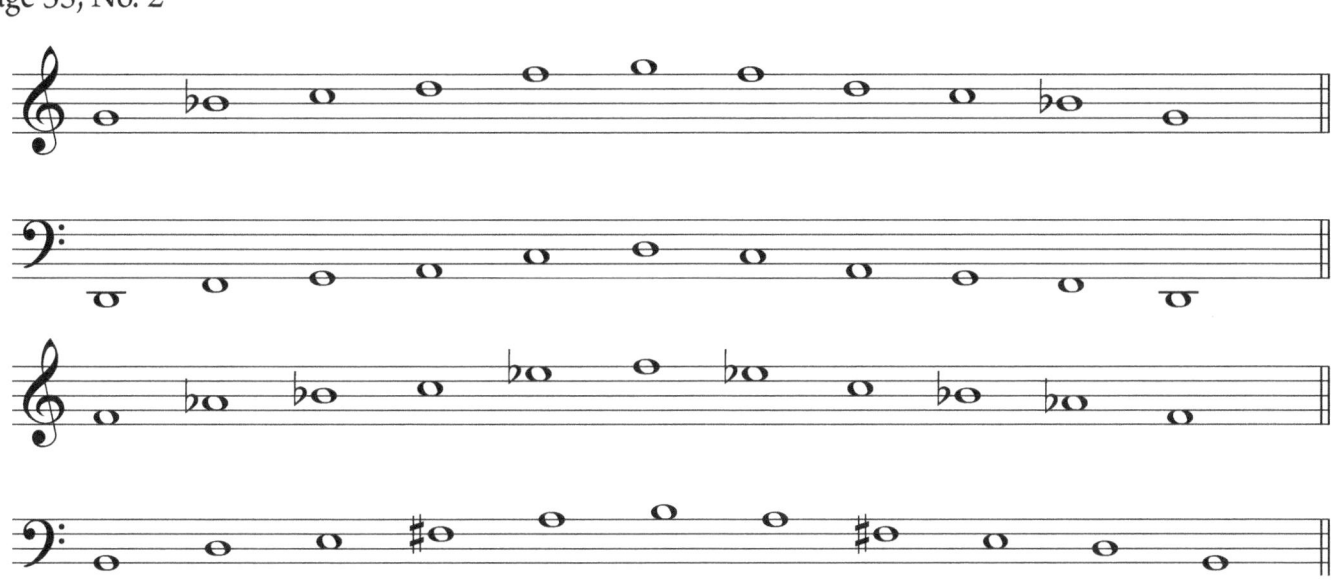

Page 36, No. 1

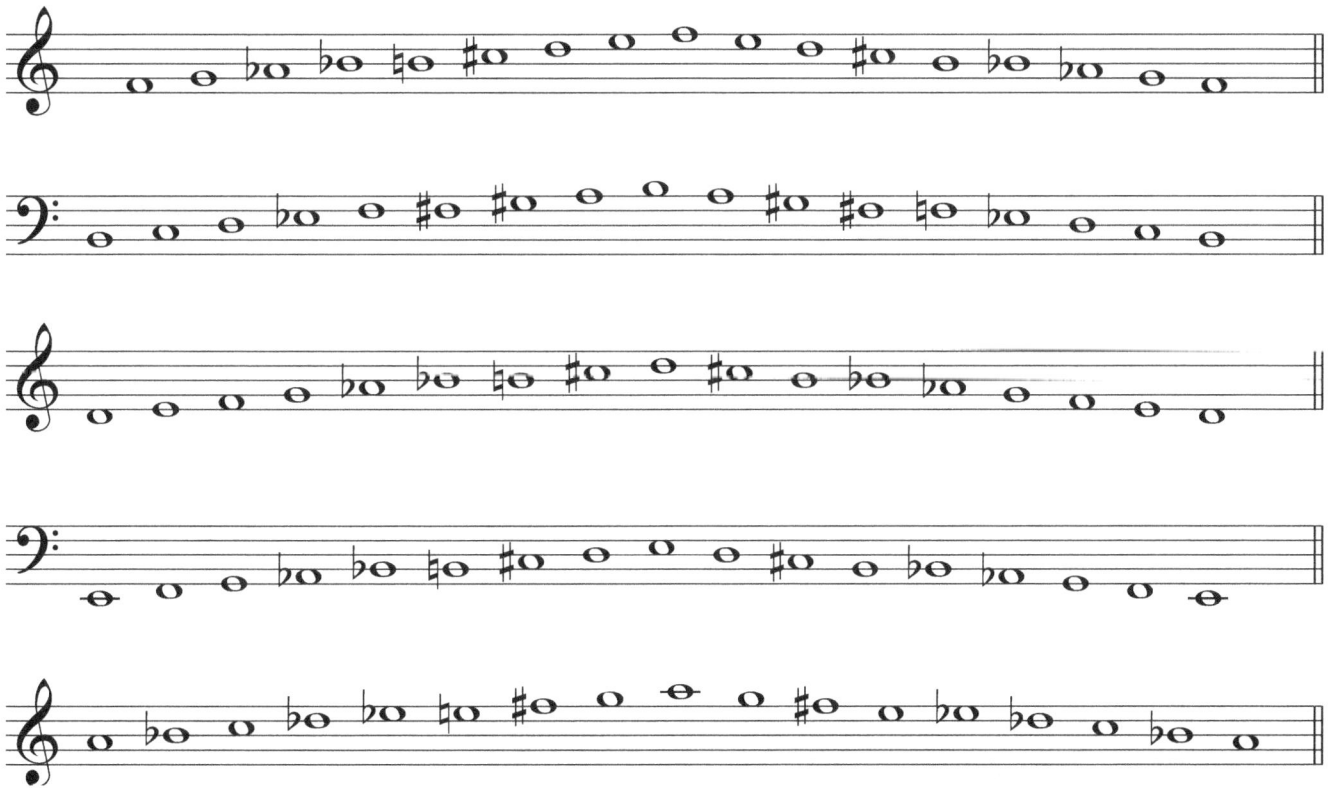

Intermediate

Page 37, No. 1

F major
E harmonic minor
E♭ major
D melodic minor
C blues
F♯ whole tone
F♯ major pentatonic
D minor pentatonic

Page 38, No. 2

E♭ octatonic
F♯ chromatic
C natural minor
D♭ major
A blues
C whole tone
F octatonic
G minor pentatonic

Page 42, No. 1

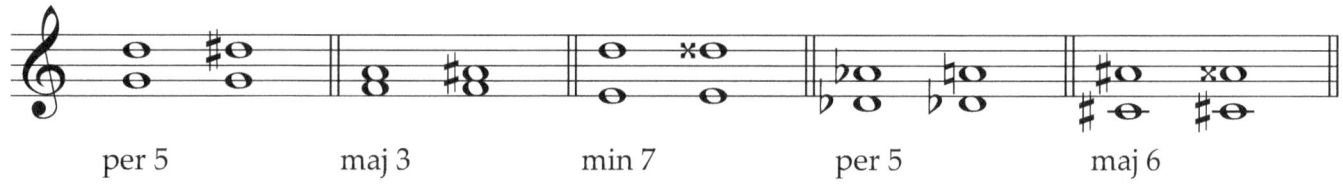

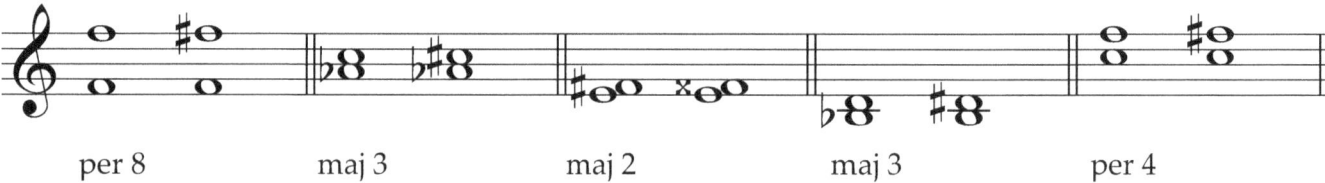

Page 42, No. 2

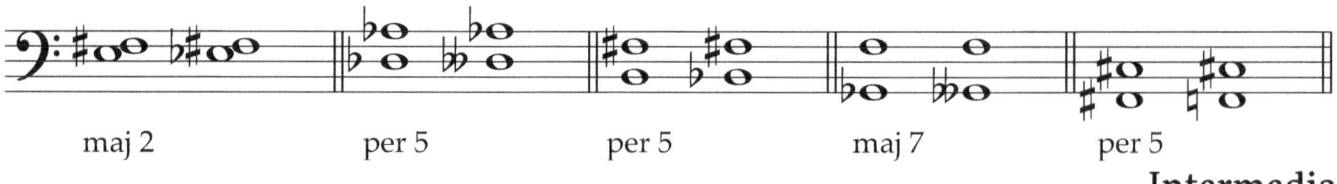

Intermediate

Page 42, No. 3

maj 3 min 6 aug 4 per 8 maj 2

maj 3 maj 6 per 5 min 7 per 5

Page 43, No. 4

per 5 maj 6 per 8 maj 3 per 4

min 7 min 3 min 6 per 5 maj 2

Page 43, No. 5

maj 3 aug 4 min 6 dim 5 per 8 dim 7 aug 2

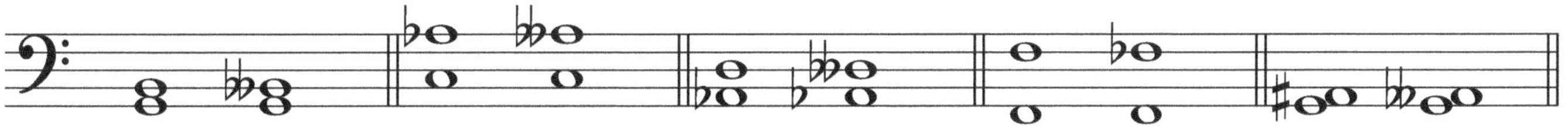

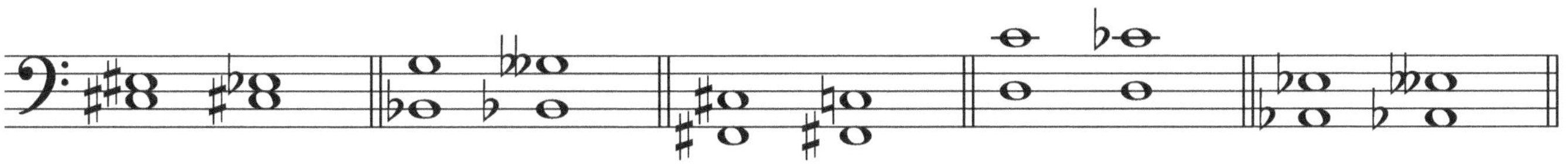

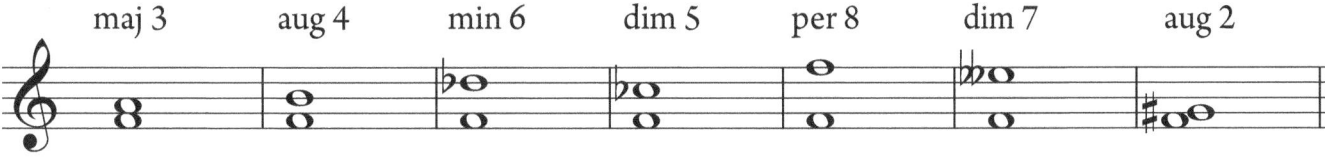

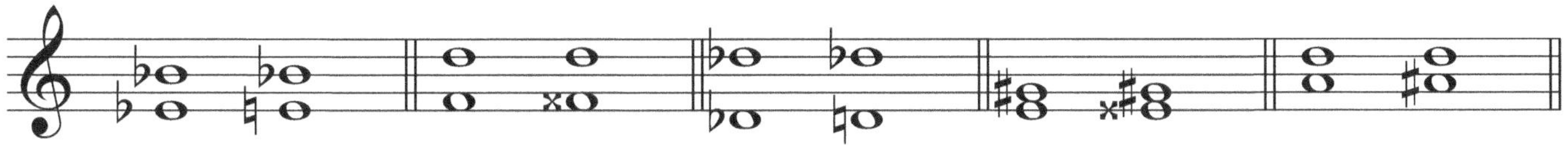

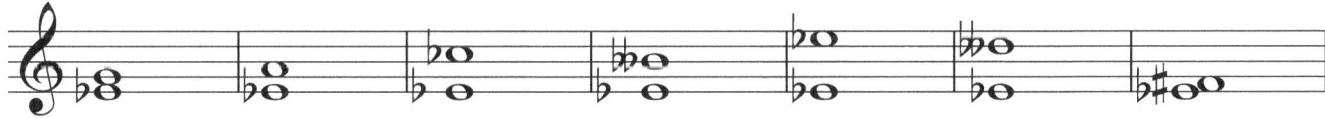

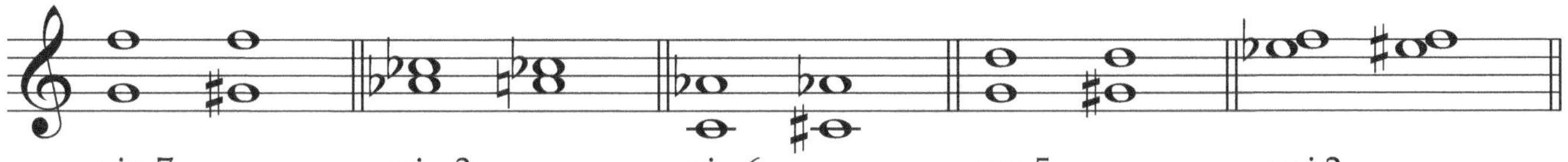

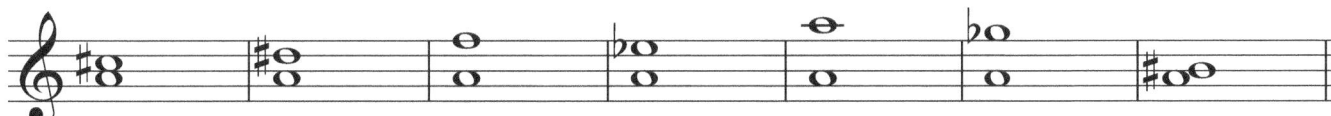

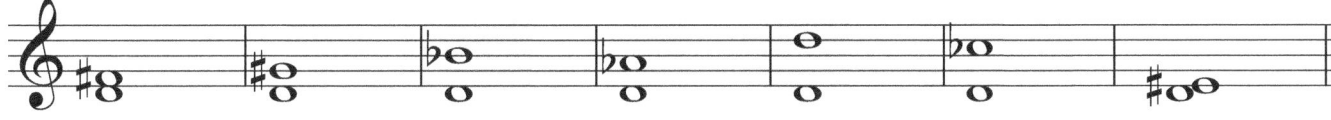

Page 44, No. 1

dim 5	min 7	maj 3	maj 7	maj 2
per 8	dim 8	aug 4	aug 3	min 6
dim 3	dim 5	maj 2	aug 5	dim 8
min 6	min 6	min 3	aug 7	aug 5

Page 46, No. 2

name: min 7 | aug 5 | min 3 | maj 2 | aug 6

inversion: maj 2 | dim 4 | maj 6 | min 7 | dim 3

name: aug 6 | aug 5 | maj 3 | dim 8 | maj 2

inversion: dim 3 | dim 4 | min 6 | aug 1 | min 7

Page 46, No. 3

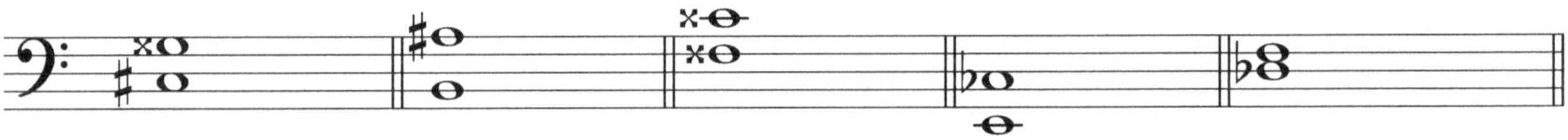

aug 5 | maj 7 | per 5 | dim 6 | maj 3

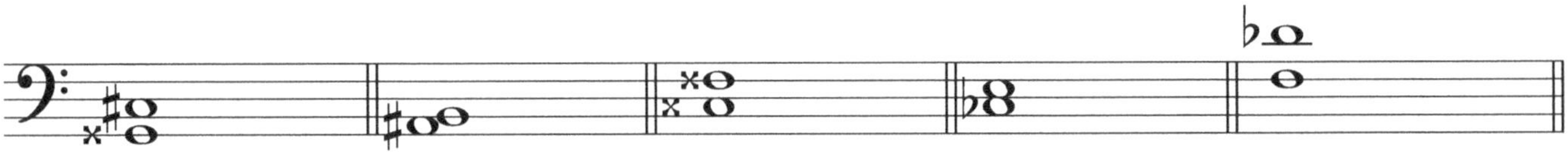

dim 4 | min 2 | per 4 | aug 3 | min 6

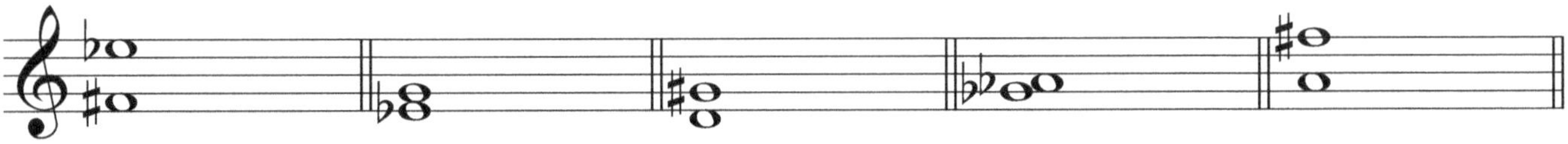

dim 7 | maj 3 | aug 4 | maj 2 | maj 6

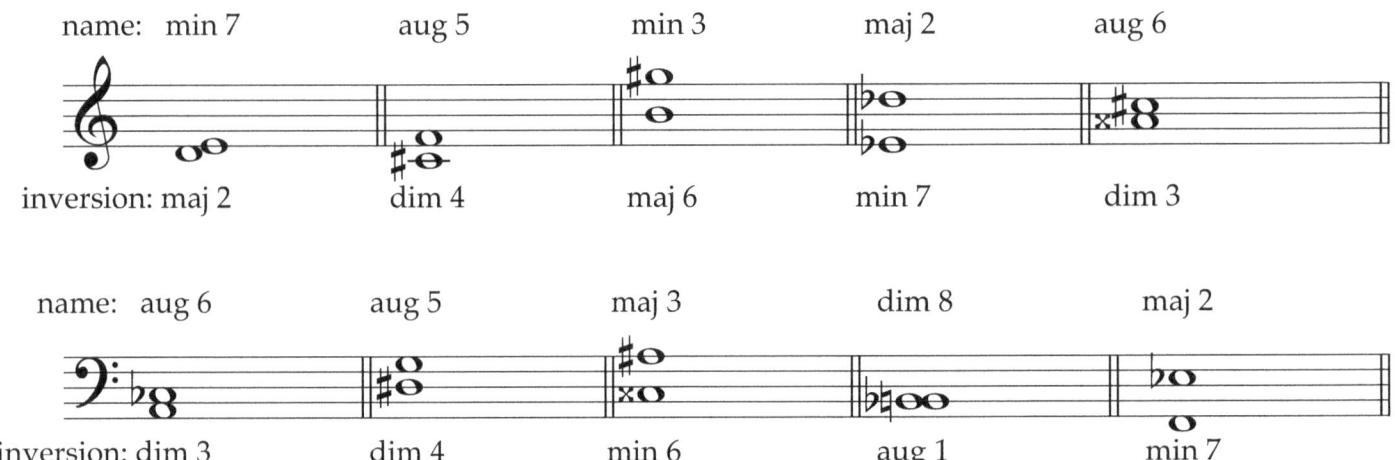

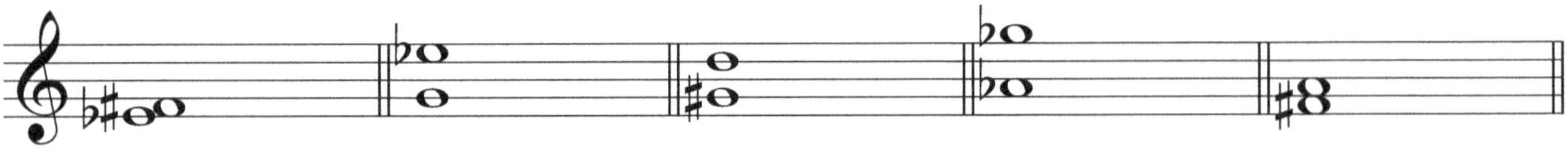

aug 2 | min 6 | dim 4 | min 7 | min 3

Intermediate

Page 47, No. 4

Page 49, No. 1

Intermediate

Page 50, No. 1

C# major	F#, C#, G#, D#, A#, E#, B#	A# minor
Gb major	Bb, Eb, Ab, Db, Gb, Cb	Eb minor
F# major	F#, C#, G#, D#, A#, E#,	D# minor
B major	F#, C#, G#, D#, A#,	G# minor
Db major	Bb, Eb, Ab, Db, Gb,	Bb minor
Cb major	Bb, Eb, Ab, Db, Gb, Cb, Fb	Ab minor

Page 50, No. 2

Page 51, No. 4

Intermediate

Page 52, No. 5

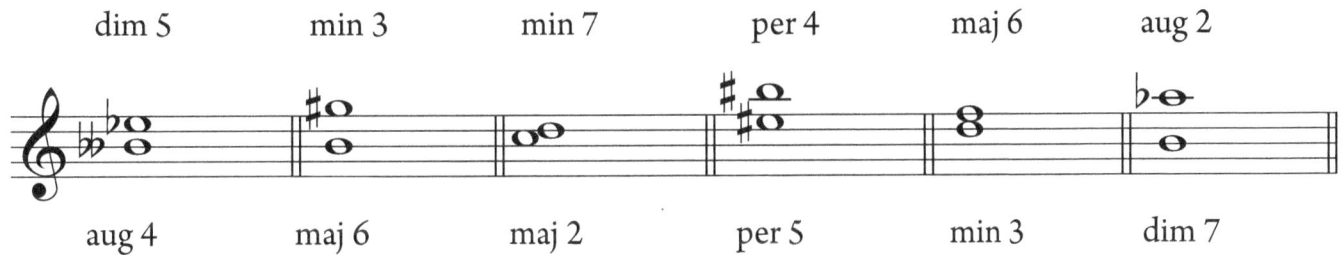

Page 52, No. 6

h f i b o n c m l p a e j k d g

Page 56, No. 1

6/8	9/8
9/4	12/16
12/4	9/4
6/8	6/4
9/8	12/8
12/4	6/4
12/8	6/8
9/16	12/8
12/16	9/8

Intermediate

Page 57, No. 2

Intermediate

Page 59, No. 1 (other options are possible)

Intermediate

Page 62, No. 1

2/4	6/8
9/16	3/4
3/4	3/2
6/4	12/8
4/2	3/8
9/16	12/4
9/8	2/4

Page 64, No. 1

Page 65, No. 2 (other options are possible)

Intermediate

Page 66, No. 3 (other options are possible)

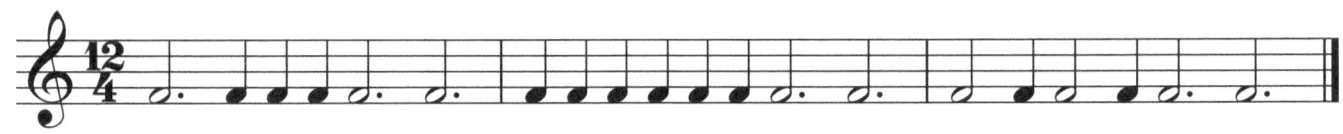

Page 67, No. 4

6/8	2/2
3/8	3/4
6/8	2/4
4/4	2/4
9/8	4/2
6/8	4/4
9/16	6/4
2/4	3/8
6/8	4/4 (2/2)
9/8	4/2

Intermediate

Page 68, No. 5 (other options are possible)

Intermediate

Page 69, No. 6 (other options are possible)

Page 70, No. 1

(a) C melodic minor   (b) subdominant
(a) F# major   (b) supertonic
(a) E♭ harmonic minor   (b) leading tone
(a) A major   (b) mediant
(a) G harmonic minor   (b) submediant

Page 70, No. 2

accelerando	becoming quicker
con moto	with movement
assai	much, very much
not troppo	not too much
sempre	always

Page 71, No. 3 and 4

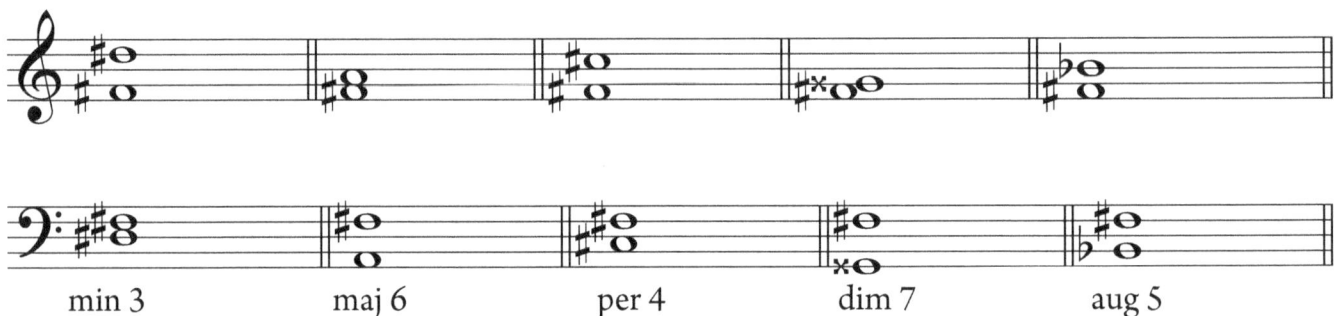

Intermediate

Page 71, No. 5

Page 71, No. 6

F major	E♭ major
E major	D major
B♭ major	A major
G♭ major	A♭ major
C♭ major	D♭ major

Page 72, No. 7

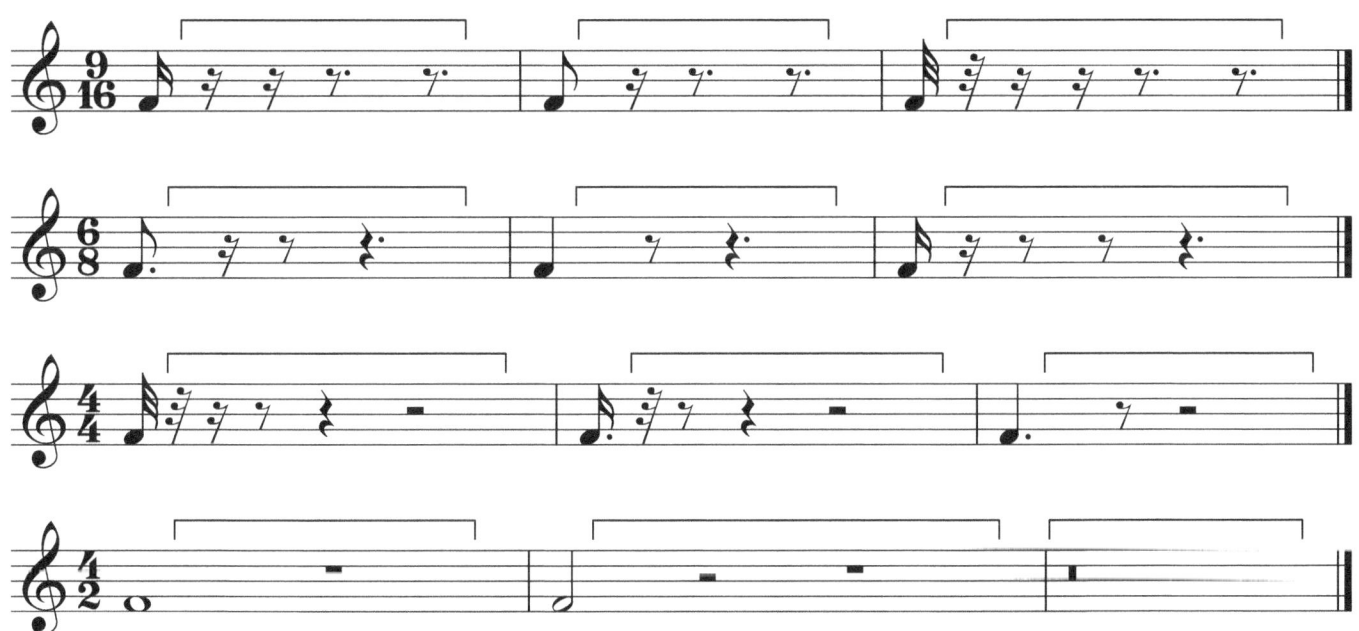

Page 72, No. 8

6/8
3/2
12/8
6/16

Intermediate

Page 74, No. 1

maj   min   maj   maj   maj   maj   maj

maj   min   maj   maj   min   min   min

min   maj   min   maj   min   min   min

maj   maj   min   min   min   min   maj

Page 74, No. 2

Page 75, No. 3

Page 75, No. 4

F   E♭   A   D   B♭   C#

G♭   A   C#   B   F   G

Intermediate

Page 76 and 77, No. 5

D	G♭	F	C♯
minor	major	minor	minor
1st inversion	root position	2nd inversion	2nd inversion

B	E♭	A	G
major	major	minor	major
root position	1st inversion	1st inversion	1st inversion

F♯	C	B♭	F
major	minor	major	major
2nd inversion	2nd inversion	root postion	root position

Intermediate

Page 79, No. 2

Page 79, No. 3

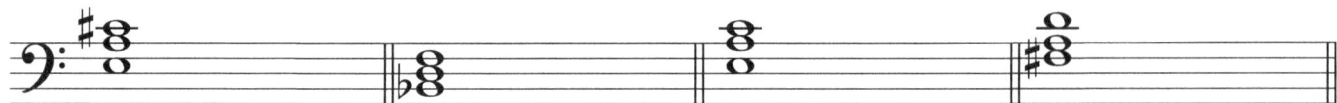

Page 79, No. 4

F	A	B♭	F#	C	A
major	minor	major	minor	minor	major
1st inver.	root pos.	2nd inver.	2nd inv.	1st inv.	root pos.
C major	G major	E♭ major	A major	B♭ major	D major
Subdominant	Supertonic	Dominant	Submediant	Supertonic	Dominant

F	D#
major	minor
Root pos.	1st inver.
F major	B major
Tonic	Mediant

Page 79, No. 5

C	F	G	F#	C	A
major	minor	minor	minor	major	major
root pos.	1st inver.	root pos.	2nd inver.	2nd inver.	1st inver.
E minor	C minor	G minor	C# minor	F minor	D minor
Submediant	Subdominant	Tonic	Subdominant	Dominant	Dominant

G	E♭
major	minor
1st inver.	2nd inver.
B minor	E♭ minor
Submediant	Tonic

Page 80, No. 1

E	F#	G	C#	F	D♭
major	minor	major	major	minor	minor
root pos.	1st inver.	2nd inver.	1st inver.	root pos.	1st inver.

B	A
major	minor
2nd inver.	root pos.

Intermediate

Page 81, No. 2

A	G	D	B	E♭	D
minor	minor	minor	major	major	major
root pos.	2nd inver.	root pos.	root pos.	2nd inver.	1st inver.
G major	E♭ major	F major	B major	A♭ major	A major
Suptertonic	Mediant	Submediant	Tonic	Dominant	Subdominant

E	G
minor	minor
Root pos.	1st inver.
D major	B♭ major
Supertonic	Submediant

Page 84 - 85, No. 1

a)	G major	b)	E major	c)	E♭ major	d)	D major
	G		E		B♭		E
	major		major		major		minor
	root pos.		root pos.		root pos.		1st inver.
	Tonic		Tonic		Dominant		Supertonic

e)	F major	f)	D♭ major
	B♭		A♭
	major		major
	1st inver.		1st inver.
	Subdominant		Dominant

Page 86 - 87, No. 2

a)	G minor	b)	C minor	c)	E minor	d)	B♭ minor
	D		A♭		E		F
	major		major		minor		major
	root pos.		1st inver.		2nd inver.		root pos.
	Dominant		Submediant		Tonic		Dominant

e)	C♯ minor	f)	D minor	g)	F minor	h)	B minor
	C♯		G		C		B
	minor		minor		major		minor
	root pos.		root pos.		root pos.		root pos.
	Tonic		Subdominant		Dominant		Tonic

Intermediate

Page 90 and 91, No. 1

A minor	B♭ major
V i	IV I
authentic	plagal
A major	D minor
IV I	V⁷ i
plagal	authentic
D major	C minor
V I	V i
authentic	authentic
A minor	G♭ major
iv i	V⁷ I
plagal	authentic
E major	F major
IV I	V⁷ I
plagal	authentic
F minor	C major
iv i	V⁷ I
plagal	authentic
E minor	D♭ major
V i	IV I
authentic	plagal
G♯ minor	D major
V⁷ i	V I
authentic	authentic

Page 93 and 94, No. 1

B minor	F major
i V	I V
half	half
B major	E major
V⁷ I	IV I
authentic	plagal
E minor	D♭ major
V i	IV V
authentic	half
D major	D♯ minor
V⁷ I	i V
authentic	half

Intermediate

E♭ major	D minor
V I	iv i
authentic	plagal
G major	A major
V⁷ I	IV I
authentic	plagal
G♭ major	B♭ major
I V	IV I
half	plagal
G♯ minor	C♯ minor
V⁷ i	i V
authentic	half

Page 95, No. 1 Review Three

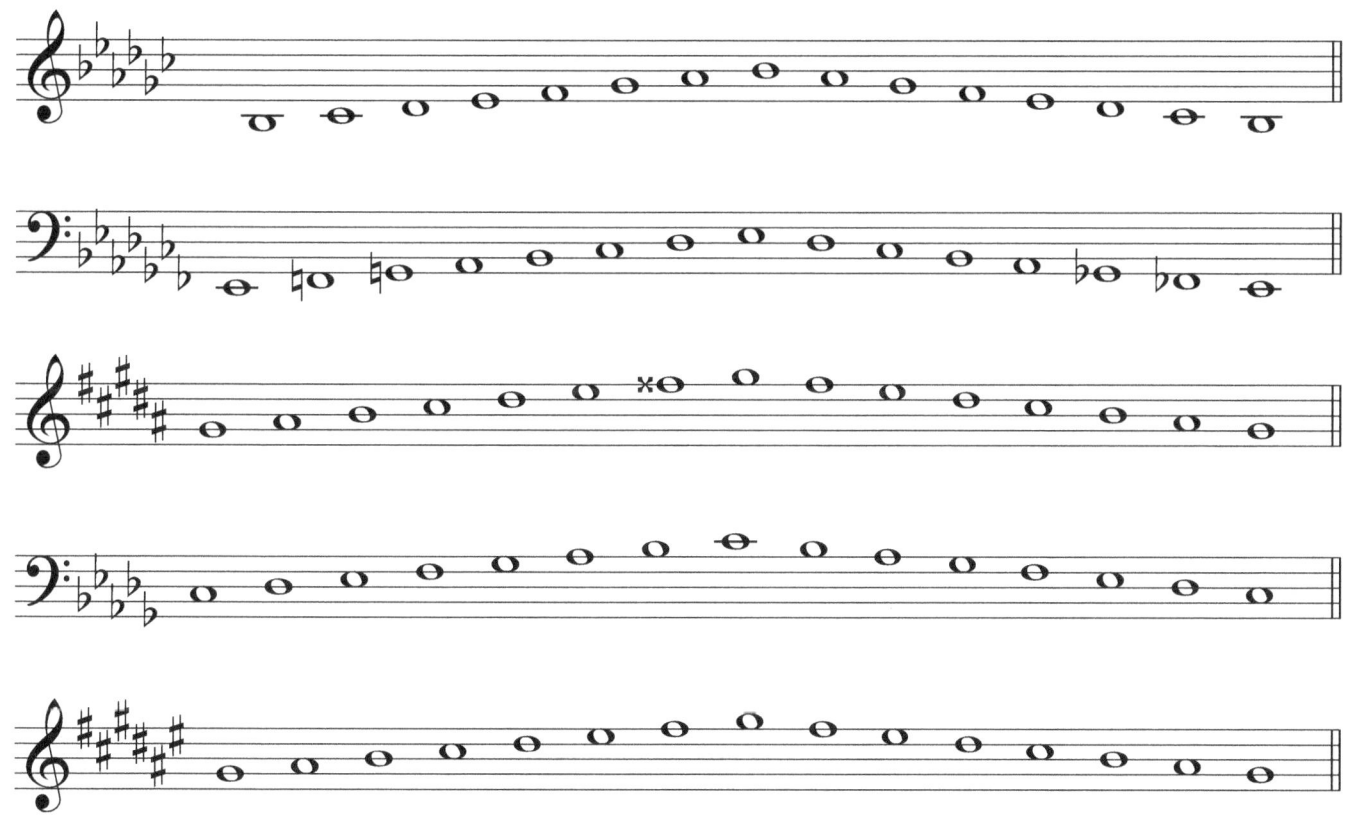

Page 95, No. 2

root:	A	C	F♯	B♭	D
type:	major	minor	minor	major	major
position:	root pos.	1st inv.	1st inv.	root pos.	1st inv.

Intermediate

Page 96, No. 3

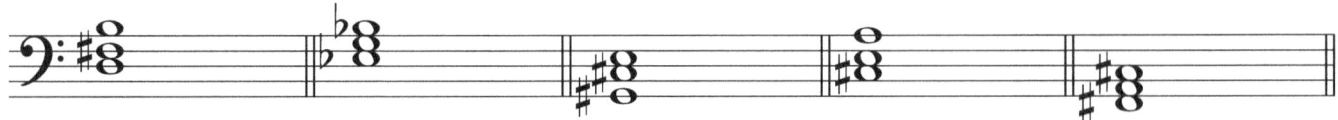

Page 96, No. 4

| A minor | V i | A major | IV V |
| | authentic | | half |

| D major | I V | G minor | i V |
| | half | | half |

| D♭ major | IV I | F♯ major | V I |
| | plagal | | authentic |

Page 97, No. 5

e m k r f g j p i l u n s d t o c b a h q

Page 99, No. 1

original key: D major

G major

F major

Page 100, No. 2

original key: E♭ major

F major

Intermediate

Page 100, No. 3
original key: A major

C# major

Page 101, No. 4

original key: A♭ major

E♭ major

B♭ major

Page 101, No. 5
original key: B major

G major

Intermediate

Page 102, No. 6

original key: F major

B♭ major

Page 103, No. 1 Review Four

D♭ major

F minor

G minor

Page 104, No. 2

original key: G major

Edvard Grieg

B major

Edvard Grieg

C major

Intermediate

D major

A major

Page 105, No. 3

c   l   o   j   i   m   k   d   e   f   g   b   n   h   a

Page 106, No. 1

(a) Define *allegretto* **fairly fast (not as fast as allegro)**

(b) Name the composer of this excerpt: **Antonio Diabelli**

(c) Add the time signature to the music. **2/4**

(d) For the chord at A, name the root: **C** type: **major** position: **root**

(e) Name the intervals at B: **min 2** C: **maj 6**

(f) Explain the sign at D: **repeat sign - repeat from the beginning**

(g) Explain the sign at E: **slur- play the note smoothly connected**

(h) Name the key of this excerpt: **C major**

(i) How many measures are in this excerpt? **8 or 16 with repeat**

Intermediate

Page 107, no. 2

Sonatina
Anh.5/1

Moderato

Ludwig van Beethoven
(1770-1827)

(a) Name the key of this excerpt. **G major**

(b) Name the composer of this excerpt: **Ludwig van Beethoven**

(c) Add the time signature to the music. **4/4**

(d) Define *moderato*: **at a moderate tempo or speed**

(e) Name the intervals at A: **maj 3** B: **dim 5**

(f) Explain the sign at C: **decrescndo - gradually get softer**

(g) Classify the chords at:
D: root: **G**   type: **major**   position: **root**

E: root: **C**   type: **major**   position: **2nd inversion**

(h) How many measures are in this excerpt? **8**

Intermediate

Page 108, No. 3

Study

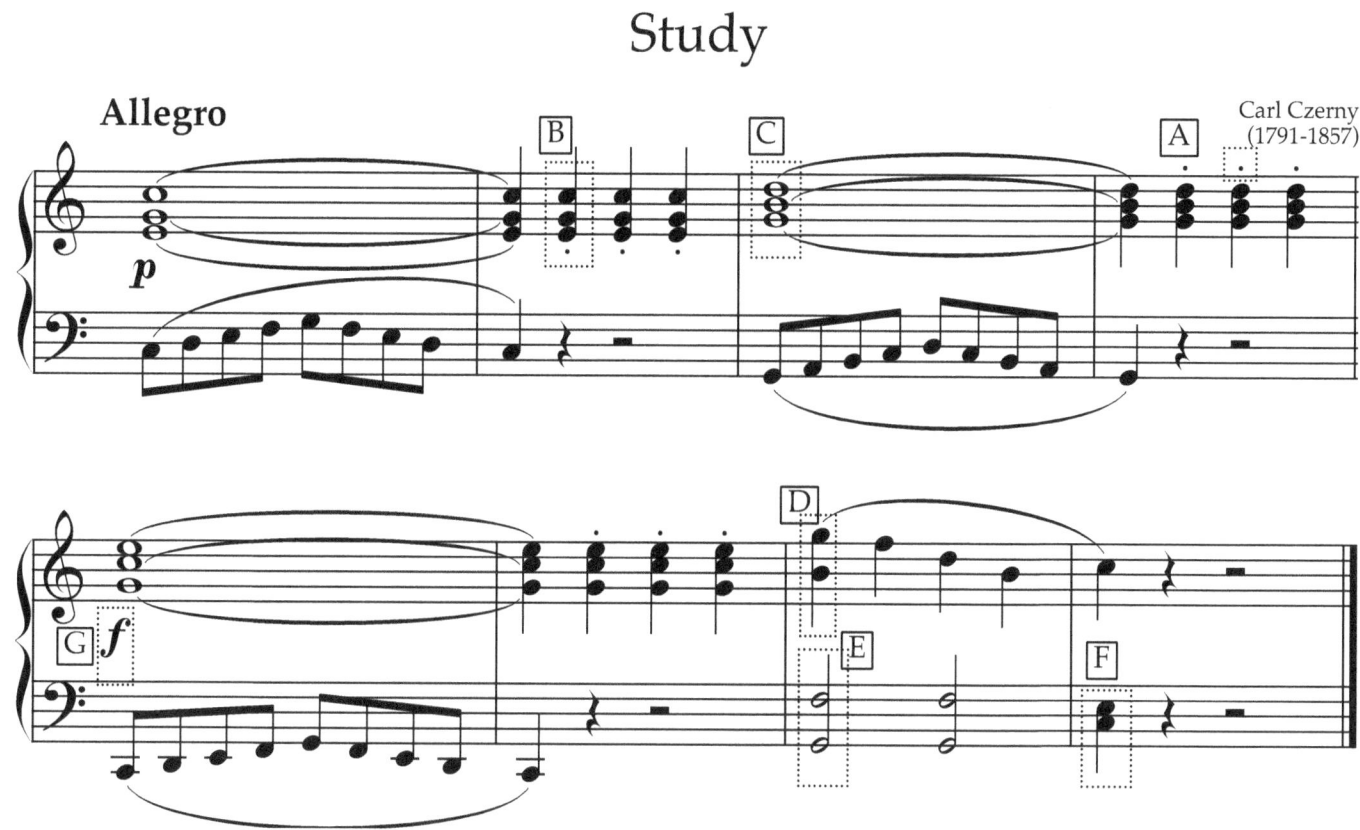

(a) Name the key of this excerpt. **C major**

(b) Name the composer of this excerpt: **Carl Czerny**

(c) Add the time signature to the music. **4/4**

(d) Define *allegro*: **fast**

(e) Explain the sign at A: **staccato - play short and detached**

(f) Classify the chords at:
    B: root: **C**   type: **major**   position: **1st inversion**
    C: root: **G**   type: **major**   position: **root position**

(g) How many measures are in this excerpt? **8**

(h) Name the intervals at D: **min 6**   E: **min 7**   F: **maj 3**

(i) Explain the sign at G: **forte - play loud**

Intermediate

Page 109, No. 4

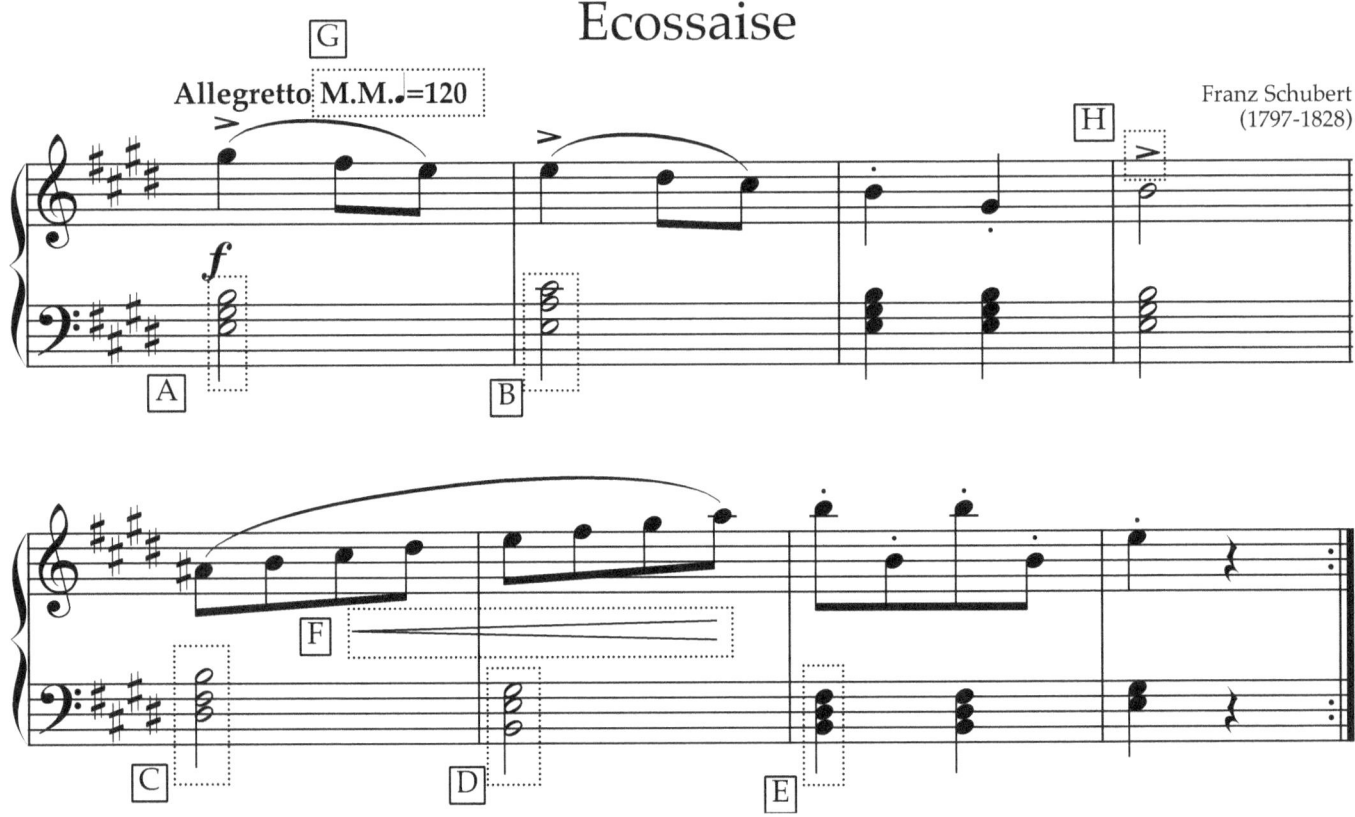

(a) Name the key of this excerpt. E major

(b) Name the composer of this excerpt: Franz Schubert

(c) When did this composer live? 1797-1828

(d) Add the time signature to the music. 2/4

(e) Classify the chords at:

    A: root: E   type: major   postion: root position

    B: root: A   type: major   postion: 2nd inversion

    C: root: B   type: major   postion: 1st inversion

    D:root: E   type: major   postion: 2nd inversion

    E: root: B   type: major   postion: root position

(f) Explain the sign at F: crescendo - gradually get louder

(g) Explain the sign at G: metronome marking Maezel's metronome

(h) Explain the sign at H: accent - play the note stronger

Intermediate

Practice Test

Page 110, No. 1

dim 5   min 3   min 7   per 4   maj 7

Page 110, No. 2

aug 4   maj 6   maj 2   per 5   min 2

Page 110, No. 3

Page 110 - 111, No. 4

C♯ melodic minor
D♭ major
D octatonic
A minor pentatonic
D♭ whole tone

Page 111, No. 5

orginal key: E♭ major
transposed key: C♭ major

Franz Schubert

Page 112, No. 6

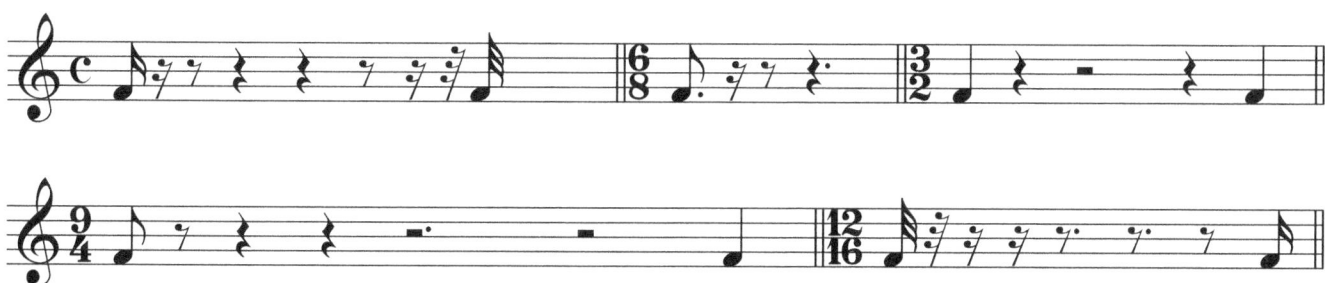

Intermediate

Page 112, No. 7

| 4/2 | 9/16 | 3/4 |
| 9/8 | 2/2 (4/4) | |

Page 112, No. 8

key: B♭ major   I   V   key: C♯ minor   V   i
cadence: half   cadence: authentic

Page 113, No. 9

(a)   F♯ minor   G minor   D♯ minor   B♭ minor   E minor
       tonic   dominant   leading tone   leading tone   mediant

Page 113, No. 10

F♯ major

E minor

Page 114, No. 11

(a) Name the key of this excerpt. E minor

(b) Name the composer of this excerpt: Joseph-Hector Fiocco

(c) Add the time signature to the music. 2/4

(d) Classify the chords at:

     A: root: E   type: minor   position: root position
     B: root: B   type: major   position: 1st inversion

(e) Name the intervals at C: per 8   D: maj 6
     E: maj 6   F: maj 6   G: maj 3

(f) Define cantabile: in a singing style

Intermediate

History

Page 127

a) Germany
b) Baroque
c) England
d) A large composition for orchestra, choir and soloists based on a religious theme.
e) 1741
f) Soprano   Alto   Tenor   Bass
g) Technique of writing music that mirrors the meaning of a piece.
h) The text "Forever and ever" is repeated over and over.
i) An opera is a play with music.
j) Classical era
k) 1791
l) Singspiel
m) German
n) A song in an opera that can be taken out and sung in a musical performance.
o) Coloratura

Page 128

The composer of the Wizard of Oz:
☑ Harold Arlen   ☐ George Gershwin   ☐ Irving Berlin

Harold Arlen was:
☐ French   ☐ Russian   ☑ American

"Over the Rainbow" was written for:
☐ Bette Davis   ☑ Judy Garland   ☐ Beyonce

The song form of "Over the Rainbow" is:
☑ AABA   ☐ ABBA   ☐ ABAB

Intermediate

a. The Baroque period occurred approximately:	☐	1600-1700	☐	1650-1725
	☐	2010-2015	☑	1600-1750
b. The following are famous Baroque composers:	☑	J.S. Bach	☑	Vivaldi
	☐	Mozart	☑	Handel
c. These elements can be used to describe Baroque music:	☑	counterpoint	☑	doctrine of affections
	☐	romantic	☑	highly ornamented
d. These are Bach's 3 main periods.	☑	Leipzig	☑	Weimar
	☐	Berlin	☑	Cöthen
e. Bach composed for the following mediums.	☑	keyboard	☑	orchestra
	☑	choir	☑	chamber music
f. How many 2 part inventions did J.S. Bach write?	☐	21	☑	15
	☐	12	☐	6
g. The 3-part inventions are also known as:	☐	sonatas	☑	sinfonias
	☐	dances	☐	fugues
h. The 2-part inventions are written for this many voices:	☑	2	☐	3
	☐	6	☐	32
i. 3 elements found in the 2-part inventions are:	☑	motives	☑	sequence
	☑	imitation	☐	monophony
j. This is the numbering system used to identify Bach's works:	☐	NRA	☑	BWV
	☐	BVW	☐	BMW

Page 137

a. Who composed Brandenburg Concerto No. 5? **Johann Sebastian Bach**

b. What genre is this work? **concerto grosso**

c. What 3 instruments are featured in this work? **violin, flute, harpsichord**

d. What is this group of instruments called? **concertino**

e. The full string orchestra in a concerto grosso is called a

☑ ripieno   ☐ concertino   ☐ oratorio   ☐ sequence

f. The form of the first movement of Brandenburg Concerto No. 5 is

☐ rondo   ☑ ritornello   ☐ sonata   ☐ binary

a. T
b. F
c. T
d. F
e. T
f. F
g. T
h. T
i. F
j. T

Intermediate

Elementary Music Rudiments Advanced Answers

Page 2, No. 1

C B G G D E F E A F

Page 2, No. 2

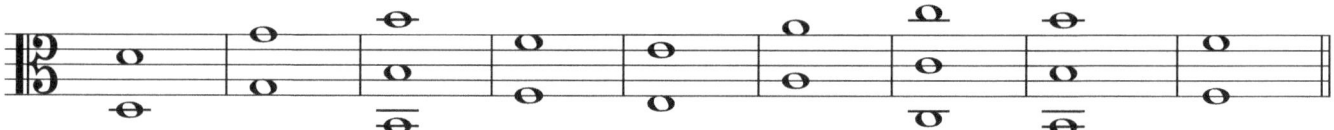

Page 3, No. 3

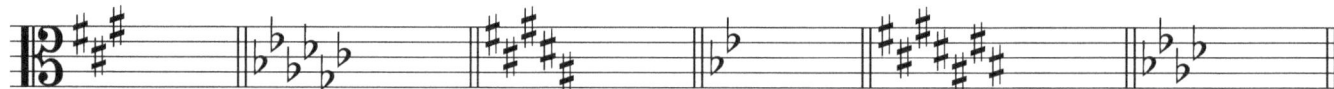

Page 3, No. 4

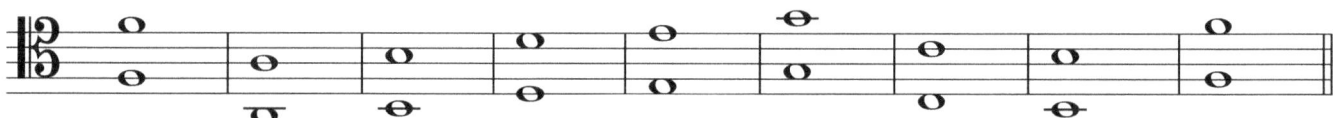

Page 4, No. 5

A D C# D♭ E F E B G# F

C# B F G D C A E D B♭

Page 4, No. 6

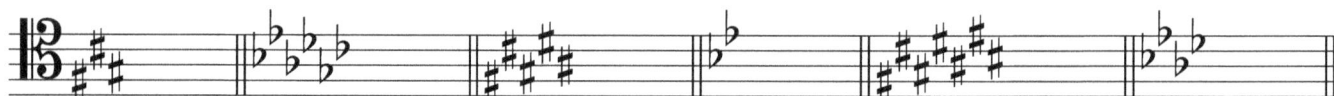

Advanced

Page 4, No. 7

Page 6, No. 1

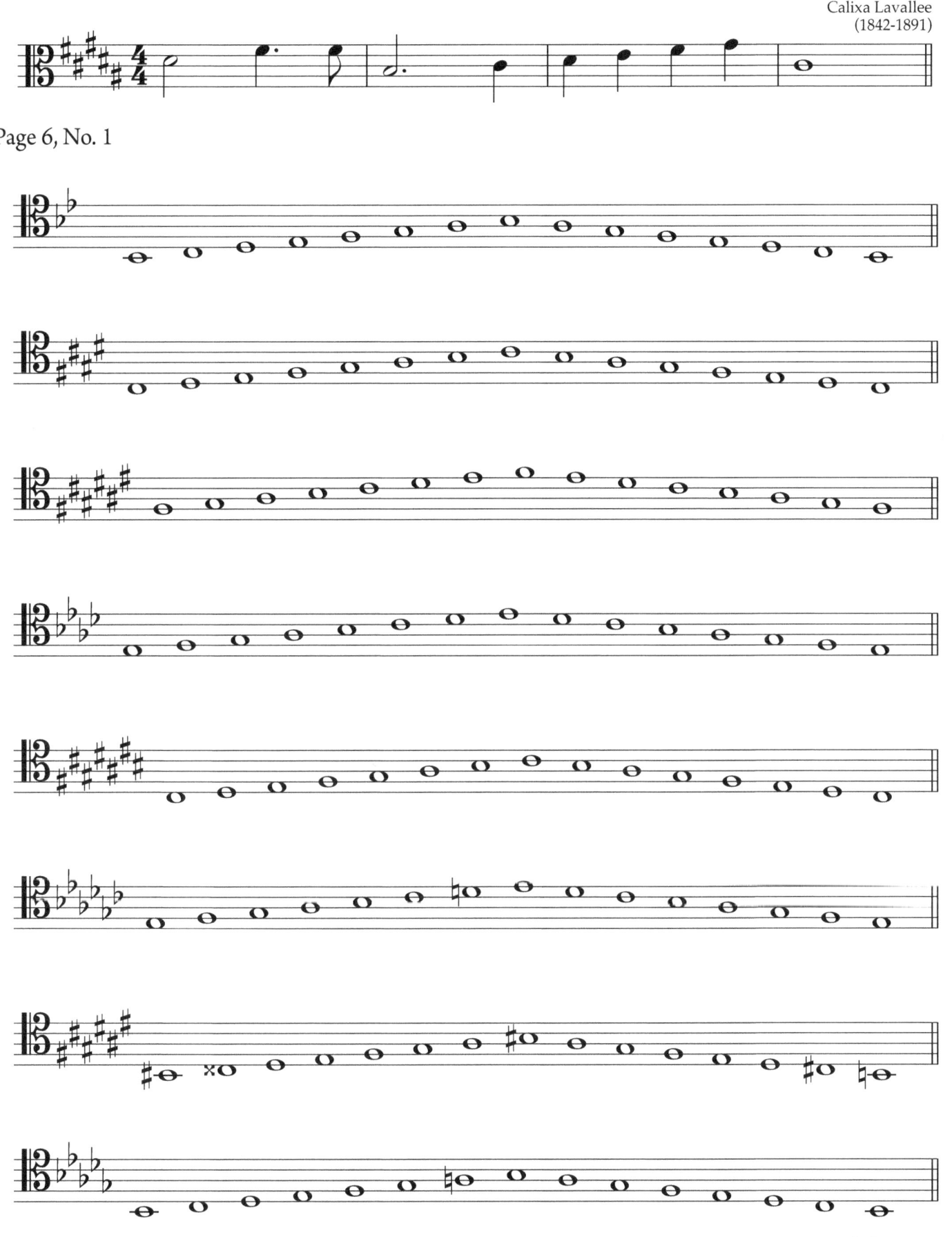

Advanced

Page 7, No. 2

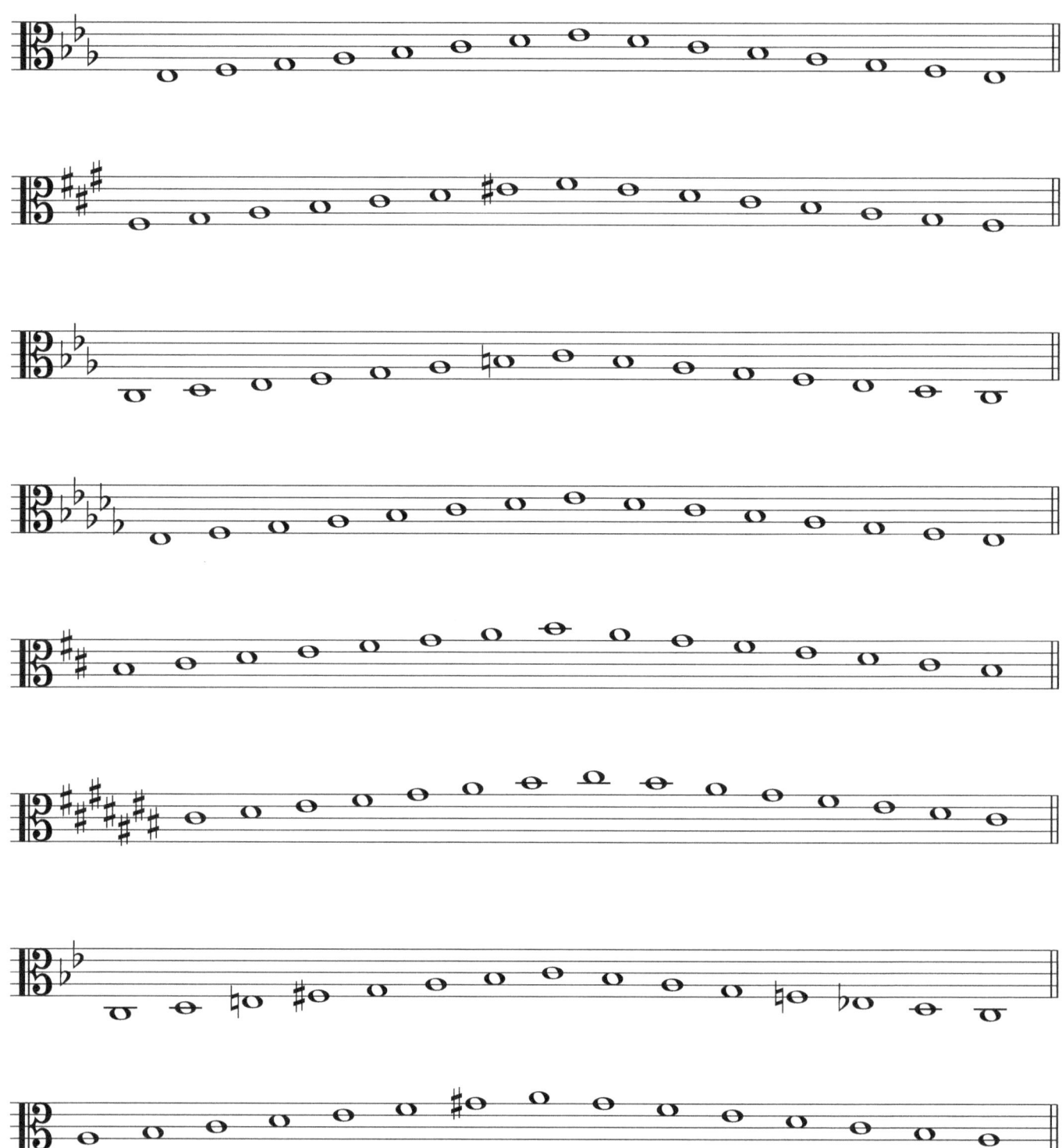

Advanced

Page 8, No. 3

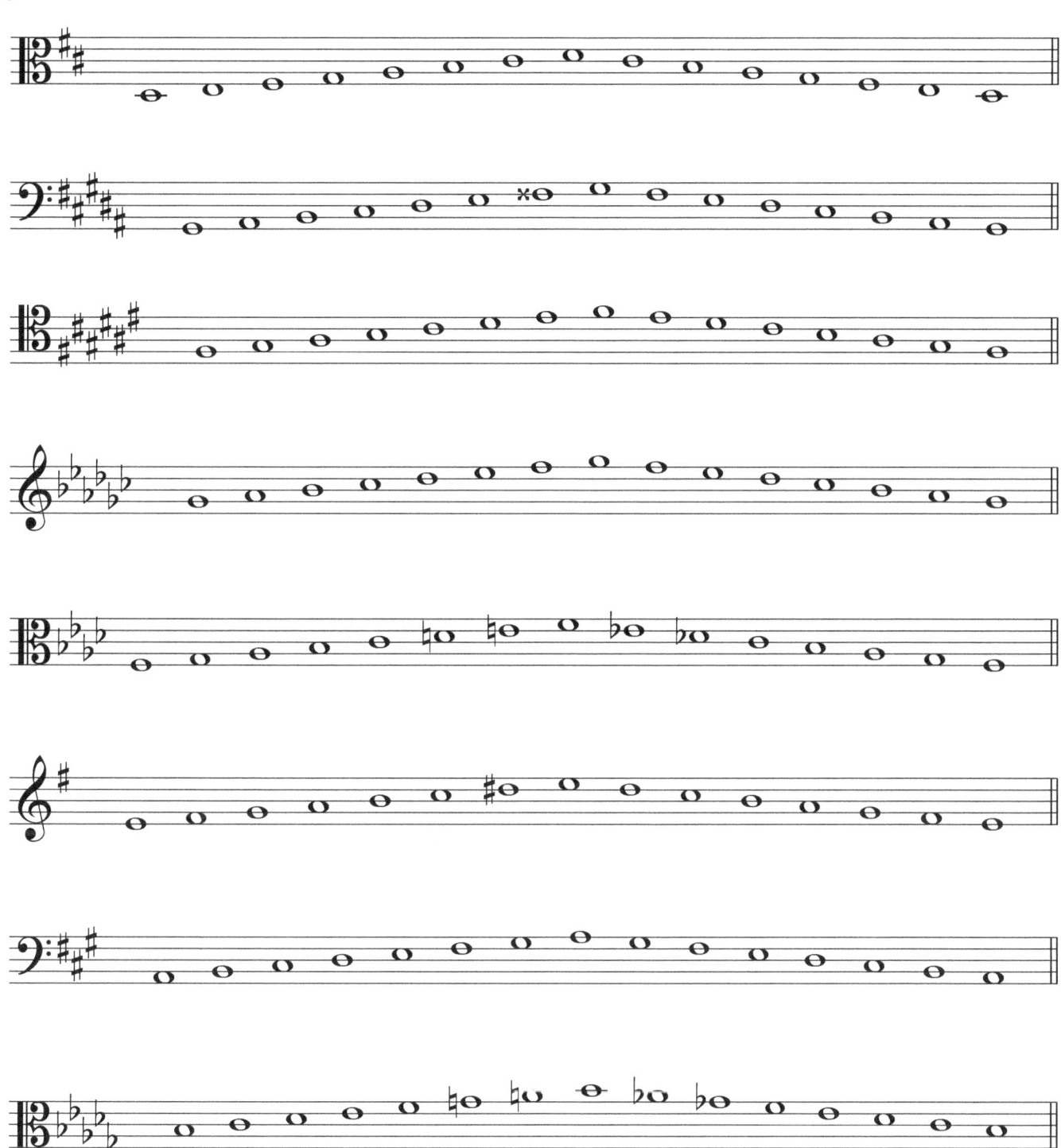

Page 11, No. 1

E♭ major
C♯ melodic minor
C minor pentatonic
E whole tone
E chromatic
E octatonic
D major pentatonic
F blues

Advanced

Page 17, No. 1

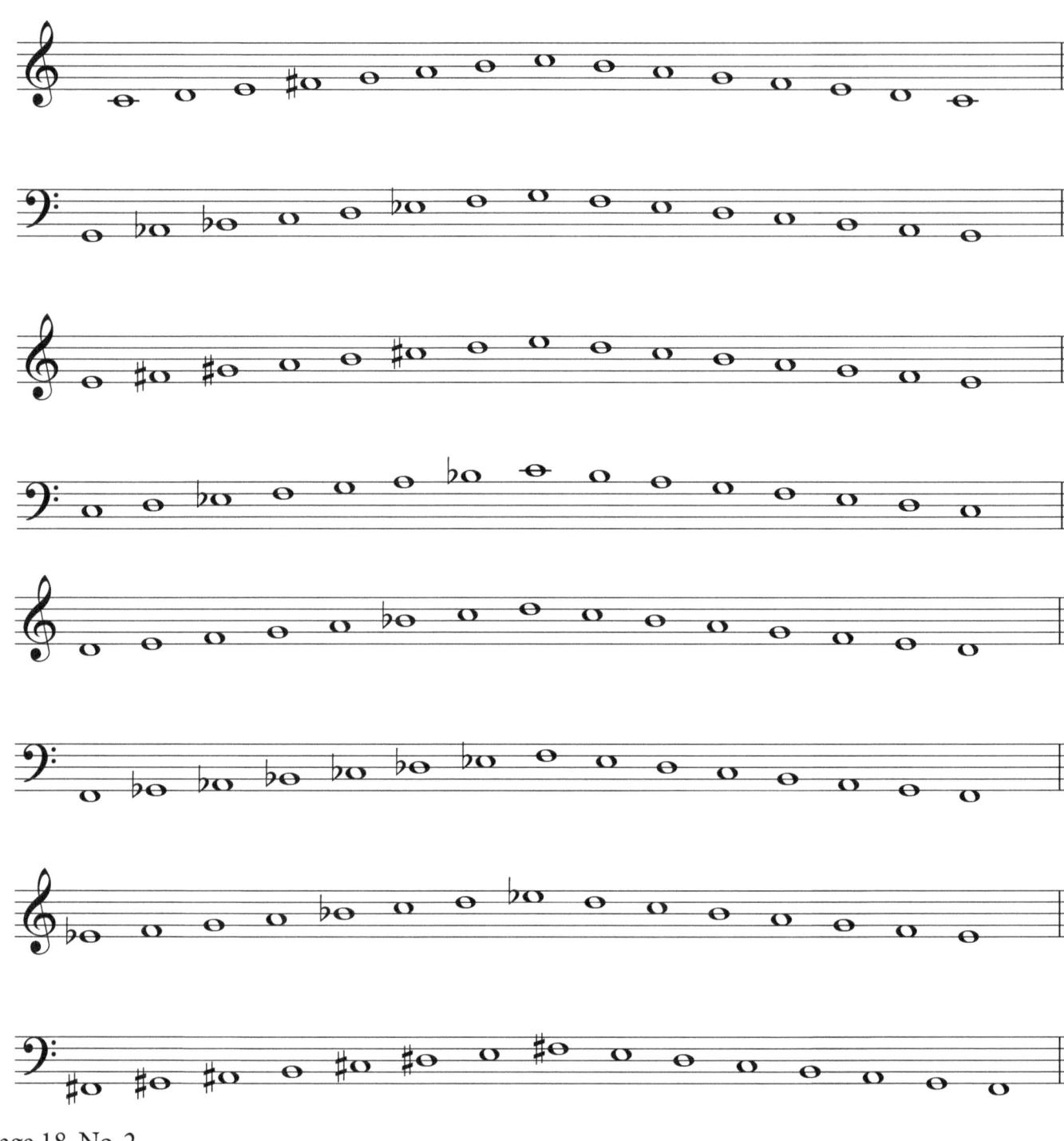

Page 18, No. 2

F Ionian
G lydian
A locrian
E♭ mixolydian
G phrygian
B♭ mixolydian
D aeolian
F# dorian
B lydian

Advanced

Page 20, No. 1

maj 6 min 3 aug 4 maj 7 dim 5 aug 2

Page 21, No. 2

Interval: aug 4 maj 2 dim 8 min 7 min 6 aug 3

Inver: dim 5 min 7 aug 8 maj 2 maj 3 dim 6

Interval: min 6 aug 7 dim 2 dim 6 dim 4 per 5

Inver: maj 3 dim 2 aug 7 aug 3 aug 5 per 4

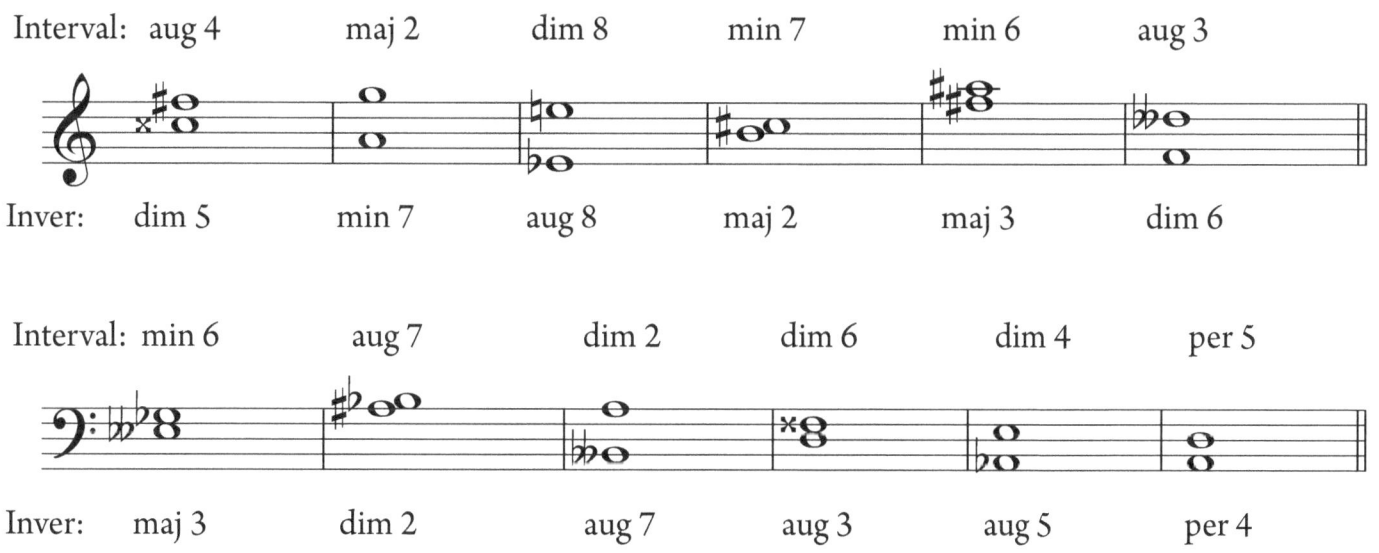

Page 21, No. 3

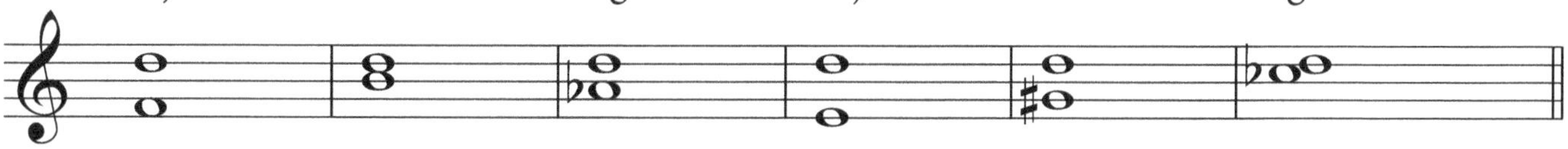

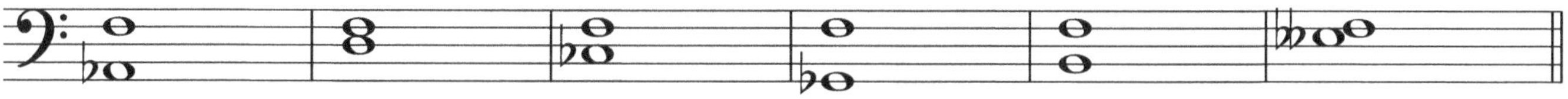

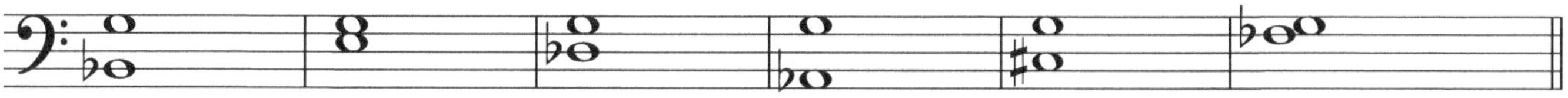

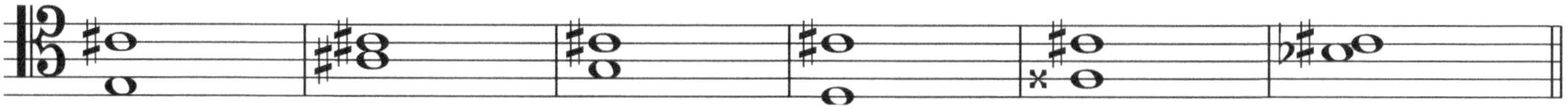

per 4 maj 3 min 2 per 5 maj 2 per 4 per 8 maj 2

Page 21, No. 4

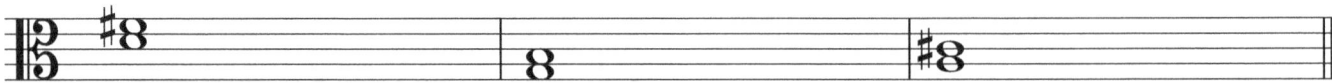

Page 21, No. 5

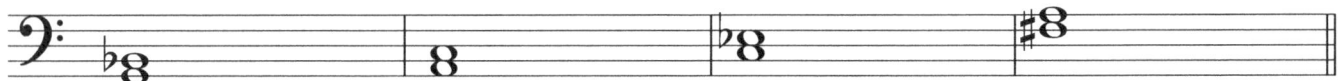

Page 21, No. 6

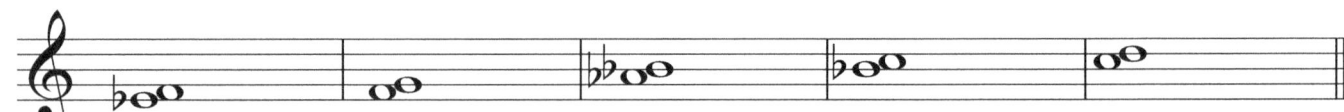

Page 22, No. 1

| min 6 | min 3 | dim 5 | aug 4 | per 4 | maj 7 |

key: F minor

| min 3 | maj 6 | per 5 | maj 2 | per 5 | maj 7 |

key: F# major

| maj 6 | maj 6 | dim 7 | maj 2 | min 7 | per 4 |

key: G# minor

Page 24, No. 1

| maj 9 | min 10 | aug 12 | aug 11 | aug 11 | per 12 |
| min 10 | maj 9 | per 11 | maj 10 | maj 10 | per 12 |

Page 24, No. 2

| dim 12 | maj 10 | min 9 | per 11 | aug 10 | per 12 |

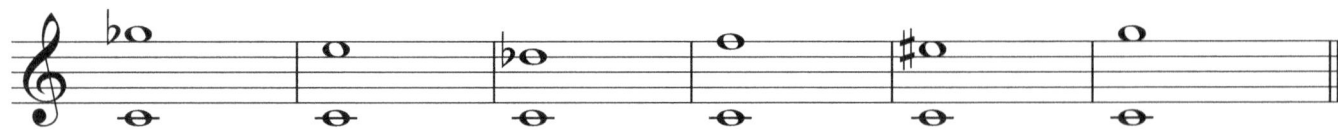

Advanced

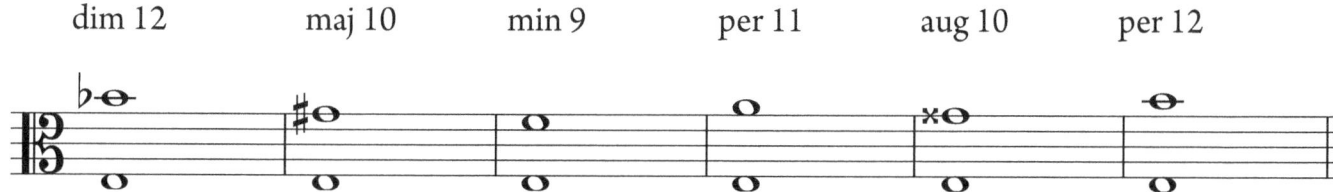

Page 24, No. 3

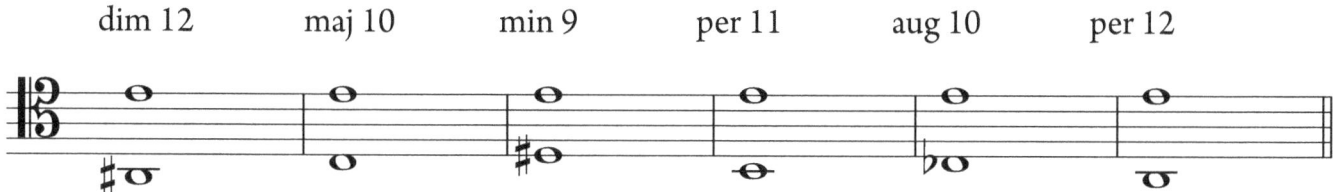

Page 25, No. 4

Advanced

Page 26, No. 1

min 7   per 5   aug 5   min 3   aug 2   aug 4

min 6   double aug 4   min 6   aug 2   min 3   dim 5

Page 26, No. 2

min 6   maj 6   dim 3   maj 7   min 6   aug 8

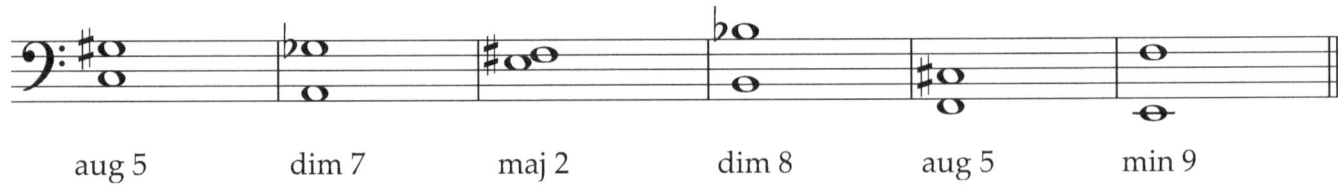

aug 5   dim 7   maj 2   dim 8   aug 5   min 9

Page 26 and 27, No. 3

per 8	per 4	min 14	maj 2	maj 3	
min 6	min 2	per 4	maj 3	dim 5	per 11
min 7	min 2	dim 7	min 6	maj 6	

Page 28, No. 1

| major | augmented | diminished | augmented | augmented | major |
| diminished | major | minor | diminished | augmented | minor |

Advanced

Page 29, No. 1

Page 29, No. 2

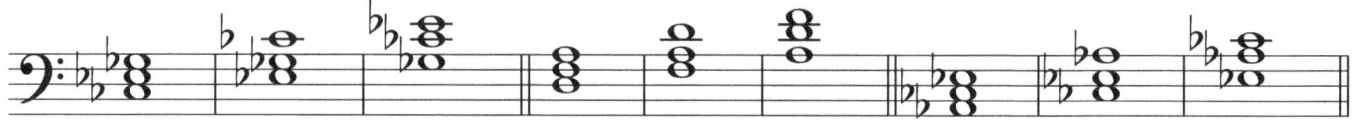

Page 30, No. 3

Page 30, No. 4

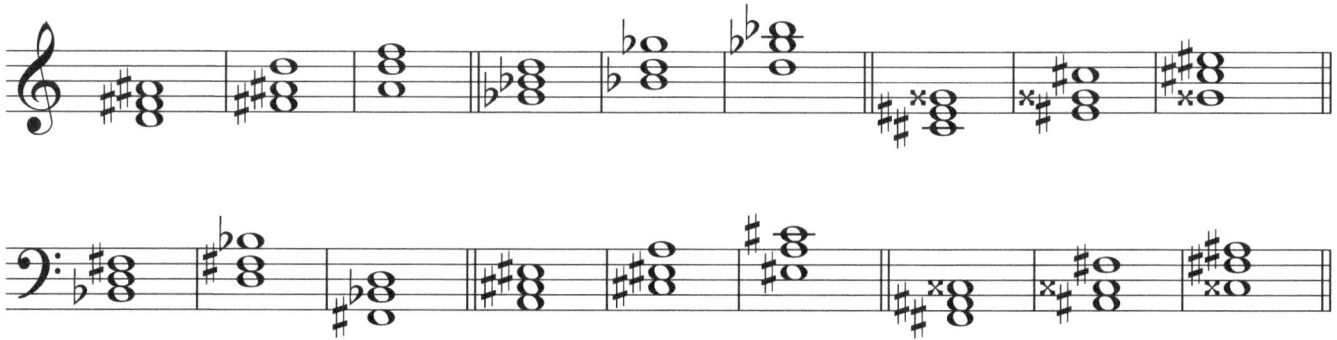

Advanced

Page 30, No. 5

F#	E♭	C	D	G	E	A♭	C#
major	minor	augmented	augmented	major	diminished	diminished	augmented
1st inver.	root pos.	1st inver.	2nd inver.	1st inver.	root pos.	2nd inver.	2nd inver

Page 30, No. 6

Page 31, No. 1

E	F#	G	C#	F	D♭	B	A
major	minor	major	augmented	diminished	minor	major	minor
root pos.	1st inver.	2nd inver.	1st inver.	root pos.	1st inver.	2nd inver.	root pos.

Page 34, No. 1

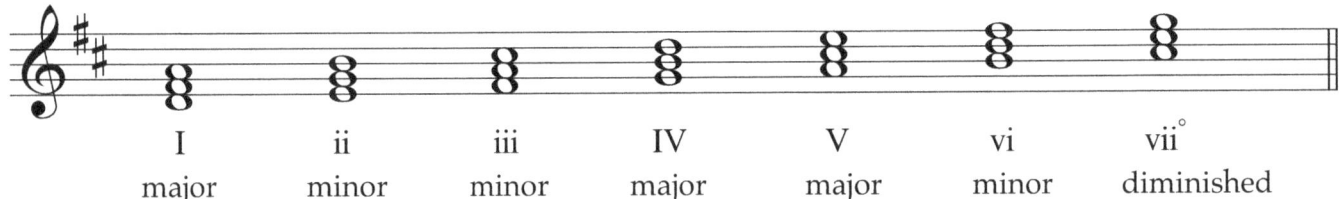

Page 34, No. 2

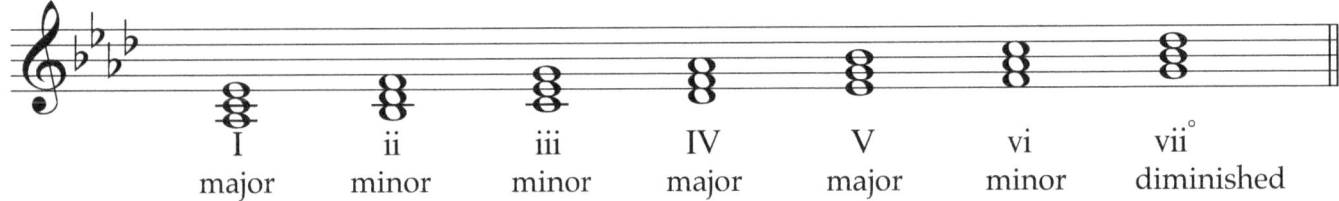

Page 34, No. 3

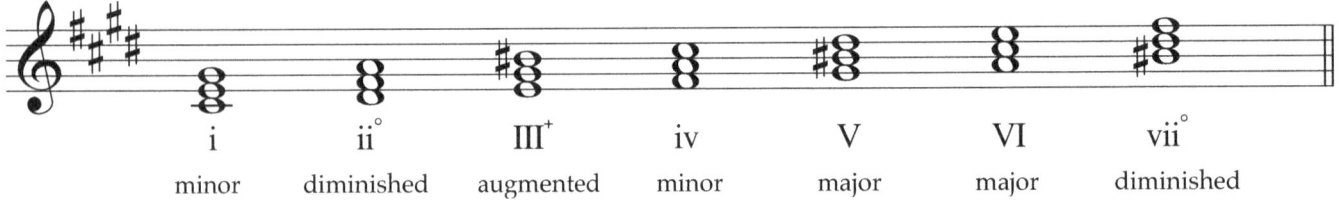

Page 34, No. 4

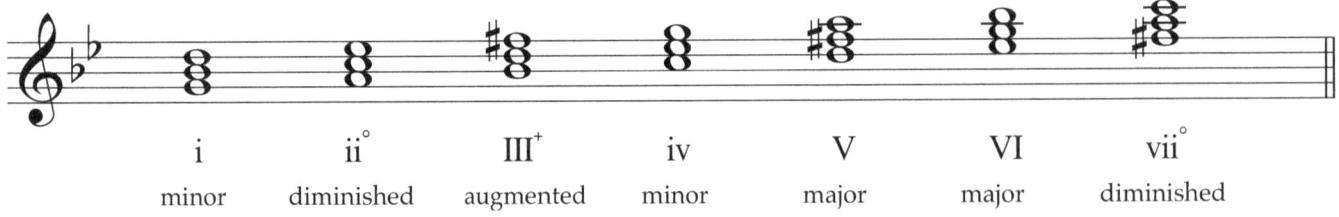

Advanced

Page 34 and 35, No. 5

A major	E major	D major	D minor	C# minor
G minor	D minor	F major	E♭ major	B♭ major
E♭ major	E♭ minor	C minor		
C# minor				
B major	F# major	E major	E minor	D# minor

Page 35, No. 6

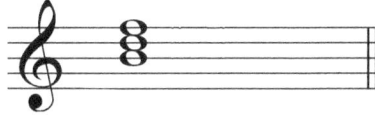

Page 35, No. 7

Page 35, No. 8

Page 36, No. 9

Page 36, No. 10

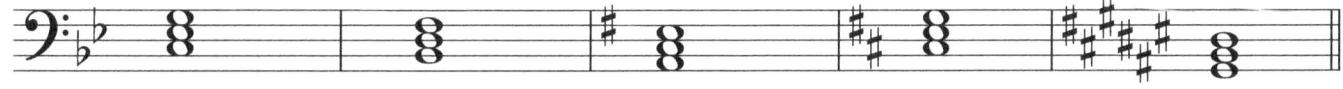

Page 36, No. 11

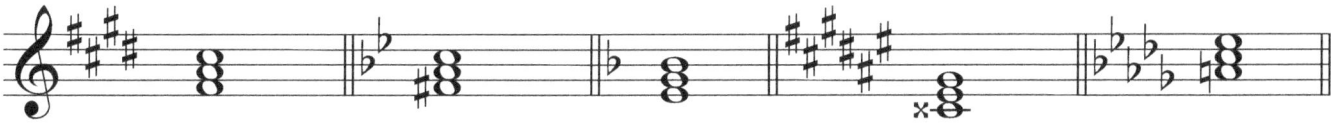

Advanced

Page 37, No. 1

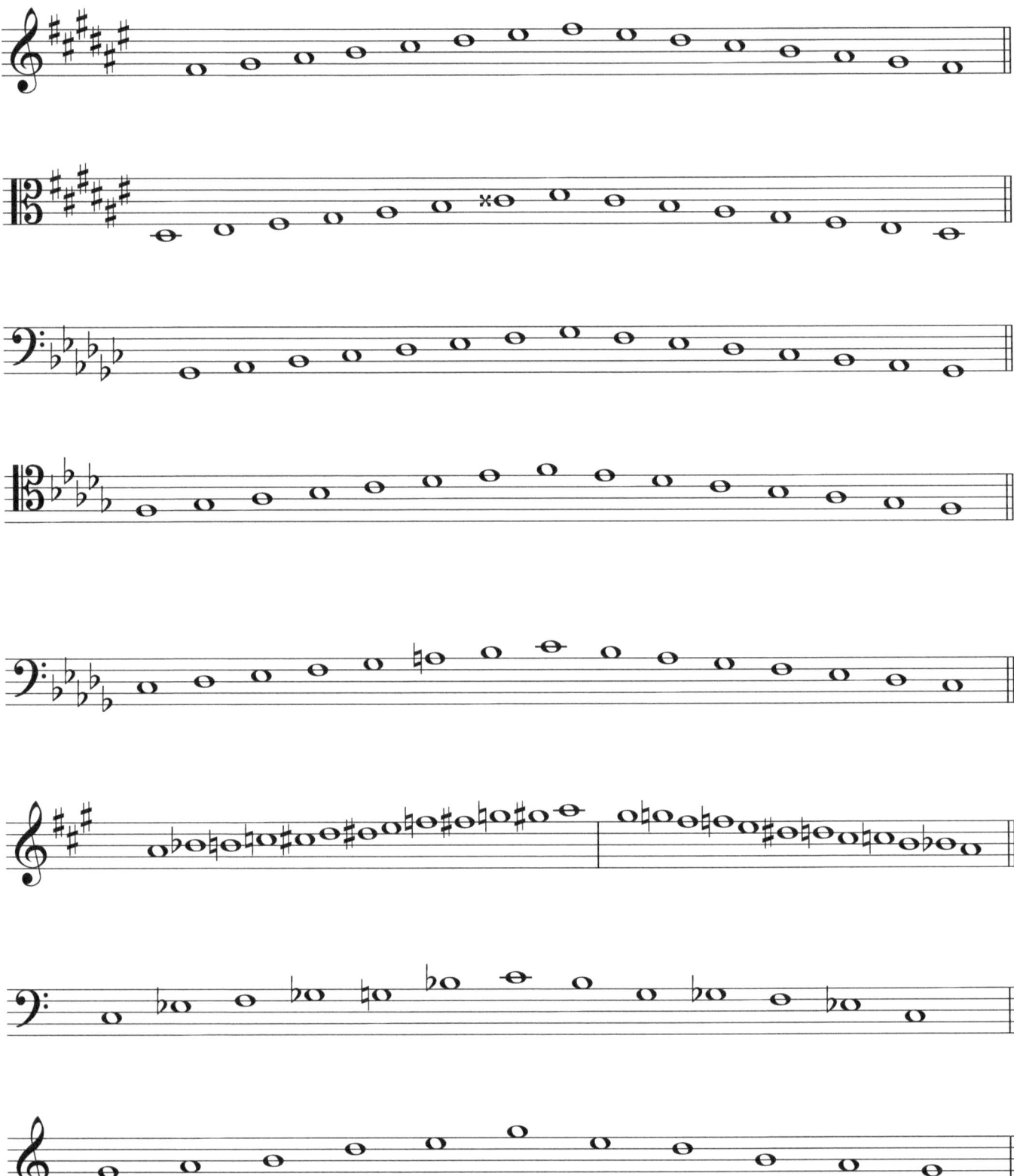

Advanced

Page 38, No. 2

aug 9   per 5   min 2   maj 10   aug 8   aug 3   min 7   per 5   min 3   aug 12

Page 38, No. 3

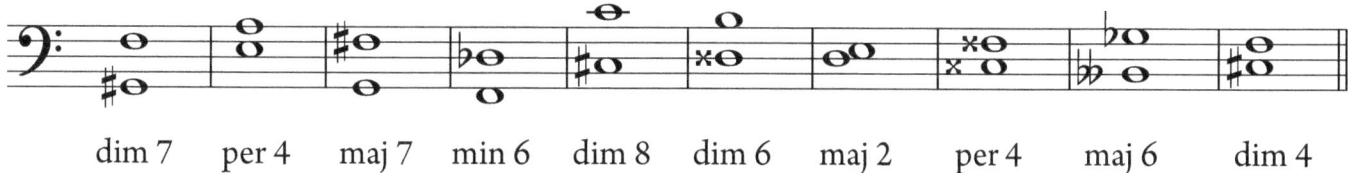

dim 7   per 4   maj 7   min 6   dim 8   dim 6   maj 2   per 4   maj 6   dim 4

Page 38, No. 4

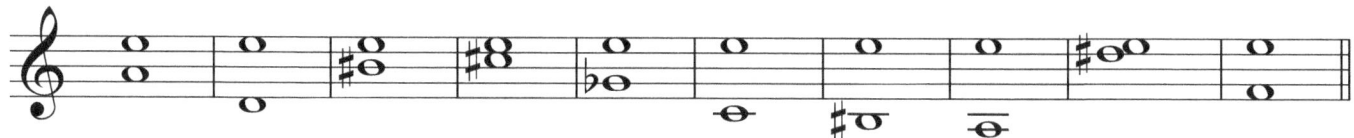

Page 38, No. 5

root:	G	A	F	D#	C♭
type:	aug	min	dim	aug	maj
position:	2nd inv.	2nd inv.	1st inv.	root pos.	root pos.

Page 39, No. 6

A minor   E minor   G major   F major   C major

E♭ major   B♭ major   A♭ major   A♭ minor   G minor

G# minor

Page 39, No. 7

j   d   e   h   k   b   i   m   l   g   a   f   c

Advanced

Page 42 and 43, No. 1

104

Advanced

Page 46, No. 1

Advanced

Page 47, No. 2

G♭ major
V   I
authentic

F♯ minor
V   i
authentic

A minor
V   i
authentic

F♯ major
V   I
authentic

E major
IV   I
plagal

C minor
V   i
authentic

E minor
V   i
authentic

D♭ major
V   I
authentic

Page 50, No. 1

G major
V   I
(GBD)   DF♯A)

C♯ major
I   V
C♯E♯G♯)   (G♯B♯D♯)

B major
IV   V
(EG♯B)   (F♯A♯C♯)

C minor
i   V
(CE♭G)   (GBD)

G minor
iv   V
(CE♭G)   (DF♯A)

E♭ minor
i   V
(E♭G♭B♭)   (B♭DF)

E major
I   V
(EG♯B)   (BD♯F♯)

C major
IV   V
(FAC)   (GBD)

Page 51, No. 2

Advanced

Page 53, 54, and 55 No. 1

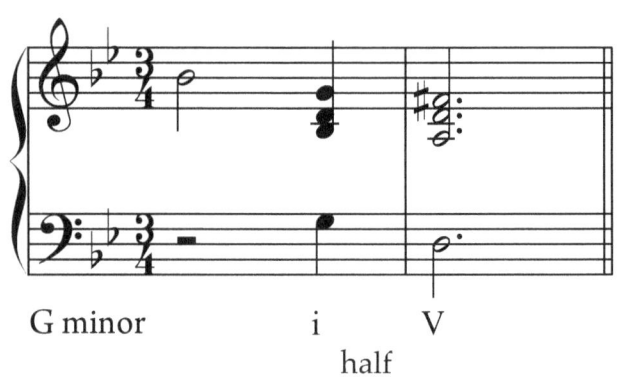

G minor   i   V
half

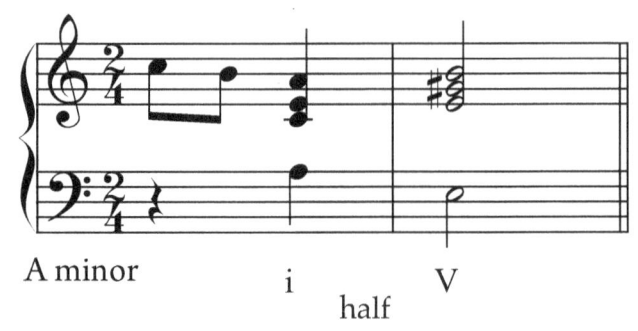

A minor   i   V
half

Page 57, No. 1

Page 58, No. 1

A	A	B	D	C	E
D major	D minor	E major	G major	F minor	A minor
root pos.	2nd inv.	1st inv.	3rd inv.	1st inv.	root pos.

B♭	D#	E	D	F#	G
E♭ major	G# major	A major	G minor	B minor	C major
3rd inv.	1st inv.	root pos.	2nd inv.	root pos.	2nd inv.

Advanced

Page 59, No. 2

G	A♭	B	D	G♯
C minor	D♭ major	E major	G major	C♯ minor
1st inv.	2nd inv.	3rd inv.	root pos.	2nd inv.

C♯	F	E	F	A
F♯ minor	B♭ minor	A major	B♭ major	D minor
root pos.	3rd inv	2nd inv.	1st inv.	1st inv.

G♯	C♯	F♯	C	A♯
C♯ major	F♯ major	B minor	F major	D♯ major
root pos.	3rd inv.	2nd inv.	2nd inv.	root pos.

Page 60, No. 1, 2, 3

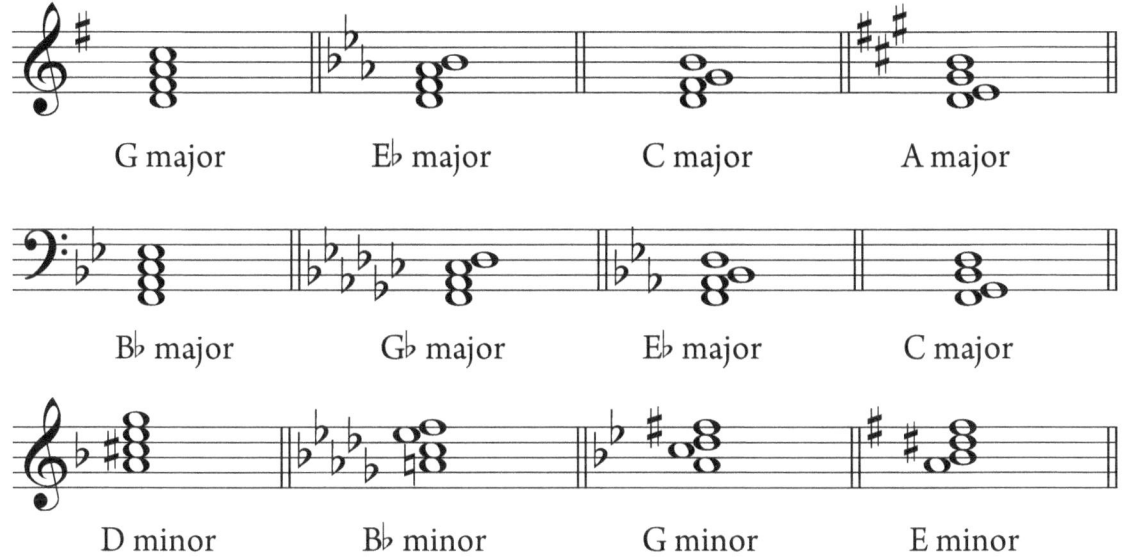

Page 61, No. 4 (other options are possible)

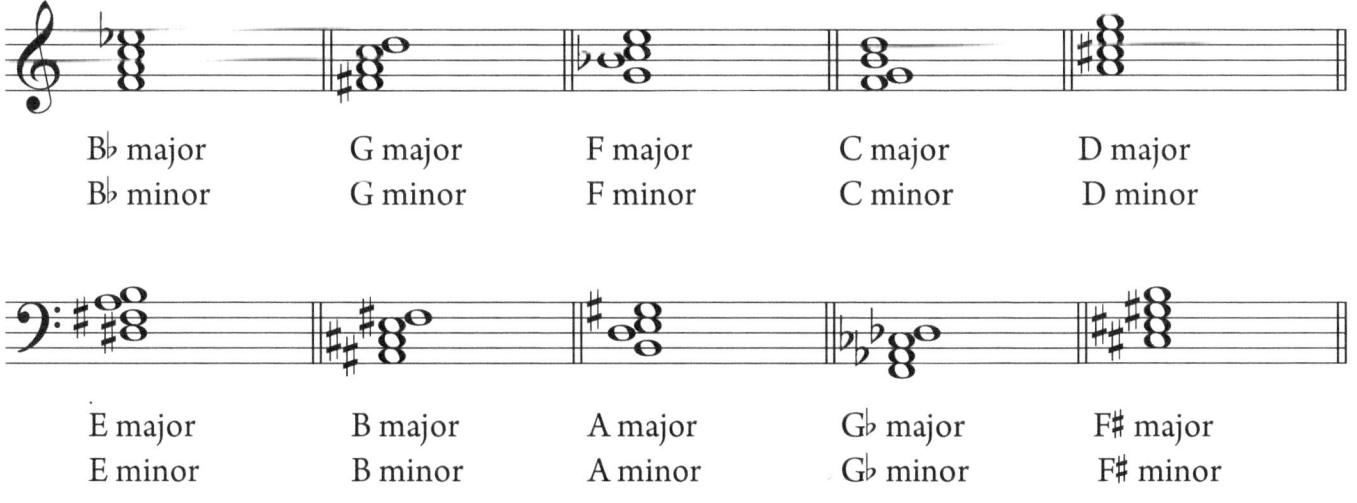

111

Advanced

Page 61, No. 5

Page 61, No. 6

Page 62, No. 7

G	B♭	D	A#	C
C major	E♭ minor	G major	D# minor	F major
root pos.	2nd inv.	2nd inv.	2nd inv.	root pos

Page 64, No. 1

vii°7	vii°7	vii°7	vii°7	vii°7	vii°7	vii°7	vii°7
E minor	G minor	B minor	E♭ minor	C# minor	D minor	G# minor	F minor

Page 64, No. 2

vii°7	vii°7	vii°7	vii°7	vii°7	vii°7	vii°7	vii°7
C minor	D minor	E minor	B♭ minor	G minor	E♭ minor	D# minor	A minor

Page 64, No. 3

Advanced

Page 67, No. 1

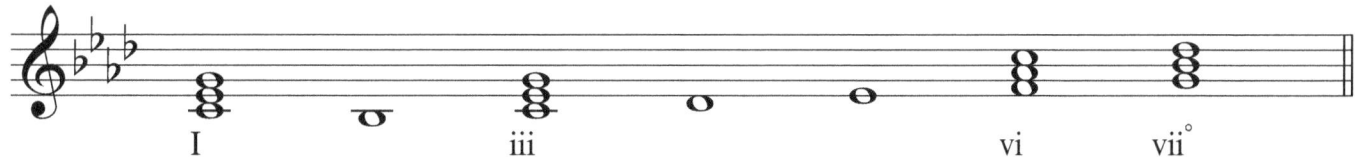

A♭ major

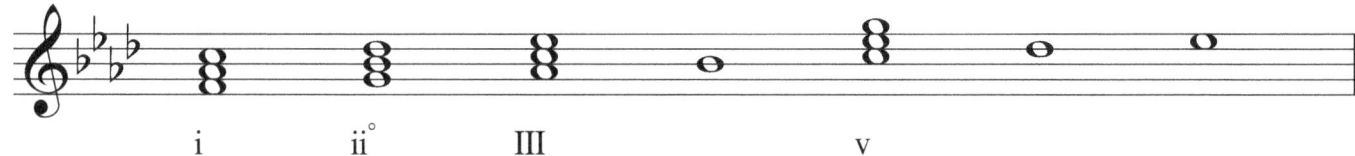

F natural minor

Page 68, No. 2

B♭	A	C	F	E♭
minor	dim 7th	dim	dom 7th	minor
1st inv.	root pos.	1st inv.	2nd inv	root pos

Scale: B♭ minor harmonic

F♯	G♯	C♯	D♯	F♯
major	minor	major	minor	major
root pos.	2nd inv.	1st inv.	2nd inv.	root pos.

Scales: F♯ major or D♯ natural minor

Page 69, No. 1

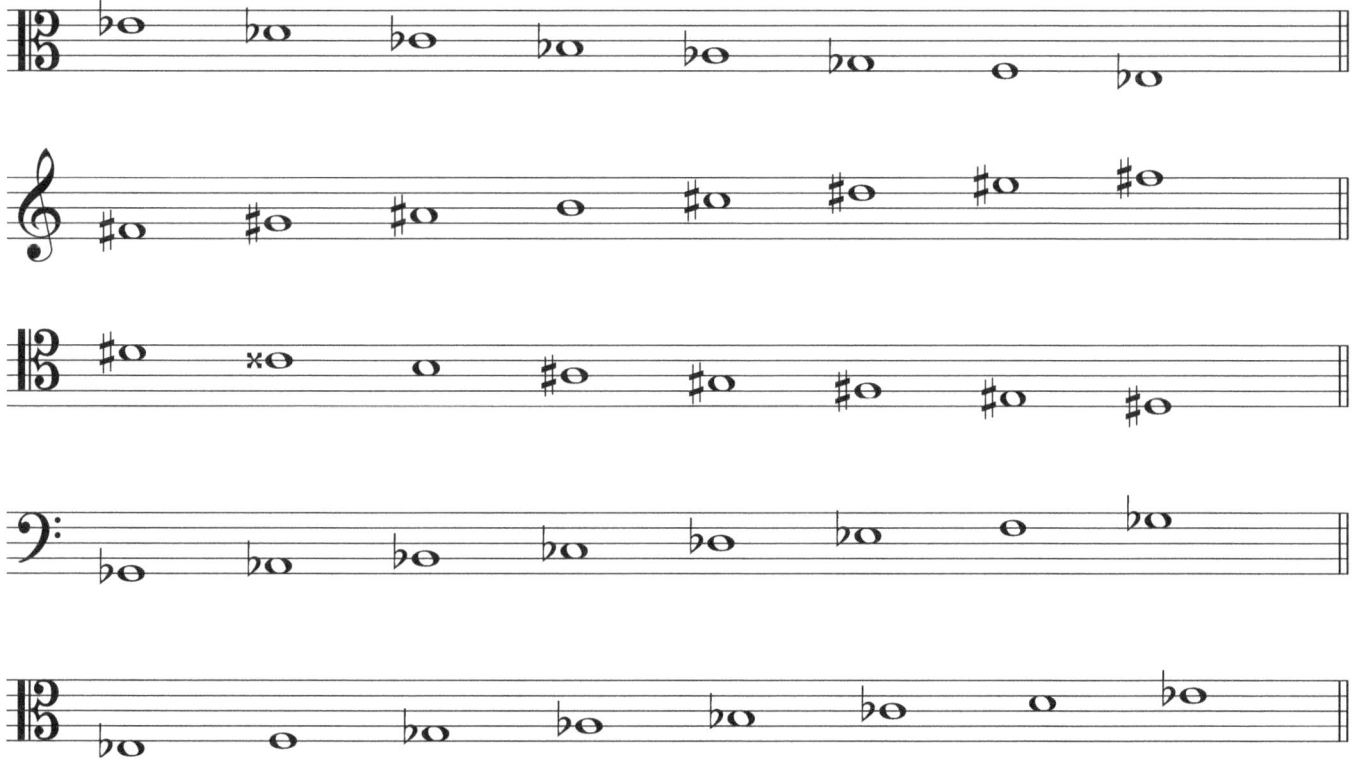

Advanced

Page 69, No. 2

per 12, maj 13, min 14, min 10, maj 6, maj 16, min 13, min 13

Page 70, No. 3

Page 70, No. 4

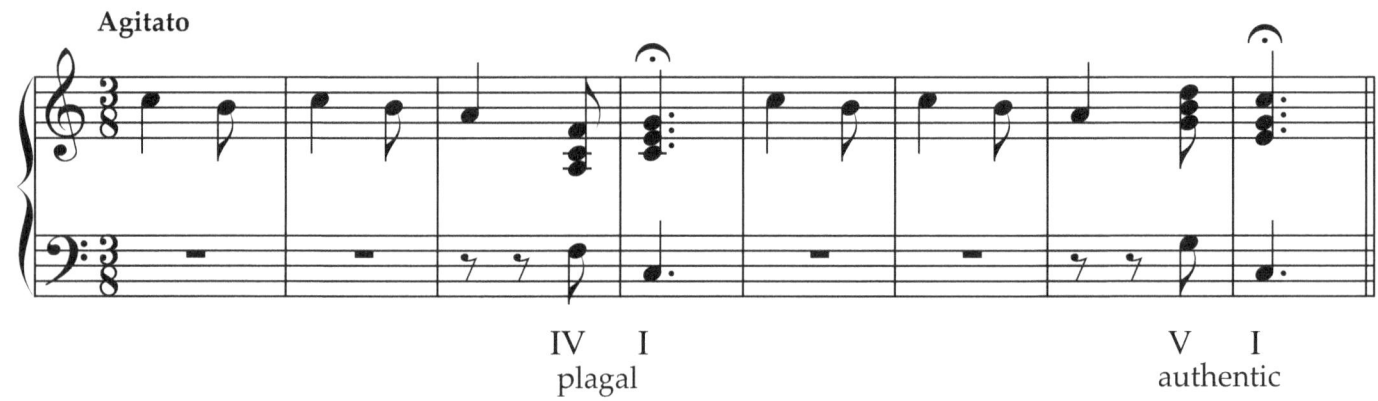

Page 70, No. 5

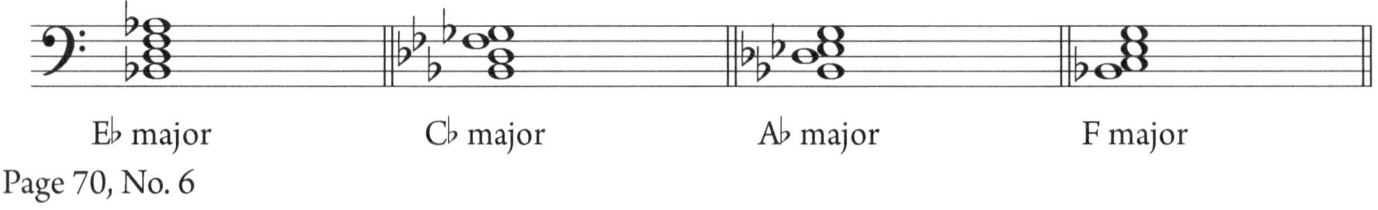

Page 70, No. 6

Page 71, No. 7

d, p, o, b, f, g, k, c, l, r, q, j, s, a, e, h, i, n, m

Advanced

Page 74, No. 1

Advanced

Page 75, No. 2

4/4	6/8
4/2	9/8
3/4	6/4 (3/2)
12/8	9/16
3/2	3/8
6/16	3/4
9/8	12/16
4/4	6/4

Page 78, No. 1

Advanced

Page 79, No. 2

7/8   5/4   10/16   5/8   11/16   7/4   5/16   9/8

Page 80, No. 3

Advanced

Page 81, No. 4

Advanced

Page 84, No. 1 (other options are possible)

Advanced

Page 85, No. 2 (other options are possible)

Advanced

Page 87 and 88, No. 1

original key: F minor
transposed key: A minor

original key: E minor
transposed key: A minor

original key: B minor
transposed key: G minor

original key: A minor
transposed key: F# minor

Page 88, No. 2

original key: G major
transposed key: C# major

original key: A major
transposed key: F# major

Advanced

Page 89, No. 3
original key: G major

transposed key: E major

transposed key: C# major

transposed key: C major

transposed key: F major

transposed key: B♭ major

Advanced

Page 92, No. 2
original key: F major
transposed key: E♭ major

Wolfgang Amadeus Mozart
(1756-1791)

Page 92, No. 3
original key: F major
transposed key: C major

Lugwig van Beethoven
(1770-1827)

Page 93, No. 1

Page 93, No. 2

| key: | F major | D♭ major | B♭ major | G major |
| key: | F minor | D♭ minor | B♭ minor | G minor |

Advanced

Page 94, No. 3

Edvard Grieg
(1843-1907)

original key: C minor
transposed key: A minor

Page 94, No. 3

Ludwig van Beethoven
(1770-1827)

original key: C major
transposed key: F major

Page 94, No. 5

largamente	broadly
mesto	sad, mournful
attacca	proceed without a break
con sordino	with mute
l'istesso tempo	the same tempo

Advanced

Page 95, No. 6

Advanced

Page 102, No. 1

Die Nacht ist kommen

Johann Sebastian Bach

Page 103, No. 2

Melody from Die Meistersinger von Nurnberg

Richard Wagner

Advanced

Page 104, No. 3

Magdalena
op.22, no. 6

Johannes Brahms

Page 105, No. 4

The Heavens are Telling

Franz Joseph Haydn

Page 106, No. 5

Christ lag in Todesbanden
BWV 279

Johann Sebastian Bach

Advanced

Page 110, No. 1

1. Add the correct time signature directly on the music. 2/4

2. What is the final measure number of this excerpt? 76

3. Name the key of this excerpt: G major

4. Name the composer of this excerpt: Joseph Haydn

5. When did the composer live? 1732-1809

6. Find one example of a **sequence** and mark it directly on the score.

7. Find one example of **inversion** and mark it directly on the score.

8. Name the intervals at A: min 6 B: min 3 C: min 3

9. Define *presto ma non troppo*: very fast but not too much

Advanced

Page 111, No. 2

Sonata
Hob XVI: 37,I

Joseph Haydn
(1732-1809)

1. Add the correct time signature directly on the music. 6/8

2. How many measures are in this excerpt? 8

3. Name the key of this excerpt: E minor

4. What is the title of this excerpt? Sonata

5. Find one example of a tritone and mark it directly on the score.

6. Name the intervals at A: min 3   B: maj 2   C: min 2

7. Classify the chords at:

   D: root: E   type: minor   position: root position

   E: root: C   type: major   position: root position

   F: root: B   type: major   position: 1st inversion

8. Name and explain the sign at G: fermata - hold the rest longer than written

Advanced

Page 112, no. 3

Rondo

Daniel Steibelt
(1765-1823)

1. Add the time signature directly on the music. 2/4

2. Name the composer of this excerpt: Daniel Steibelt

3. Name the key of this excerpt: C major

4. Explain the sign at A: crescendo - gradually get louder

5. Classify the chords at:

    B: root: C   type: major   position: root position

    C: root: F   type: major   position: 2nd inversion

    D: root: G   type: dom 7th   position: root position

    E: root: G   type: major   position: root position

6. Define *allegro*: fast

Advanced

Page 113, No. 4

L'Arabesque

Friedrich Johann Franz Burgmuller
(1806-1874)

1. Add the time signature directly on the music. 2/4

2. Name the composer of this excerpt: Friedrich Johann Franz Burgmuller

3. How many measures are in this excerpt? 8

4. Define *allegro scherzando*: fast and playful

5. Define *leggiero*: lightly

6. Classify the chords at:

   A: root: A   type: minor   position: root position

   B: root: D   type: minor   position: 2nd inversion

   C: root: C   type: major   position: 2nd inversion

   D: root: G   type: dom 7th   position: root position

7. Explain the sign at E: sforzando a sudden strong accent

8. Find an example of a **sequence** and mark it directly on the score.

Advanced

Practice Test

Page 114, No. 1

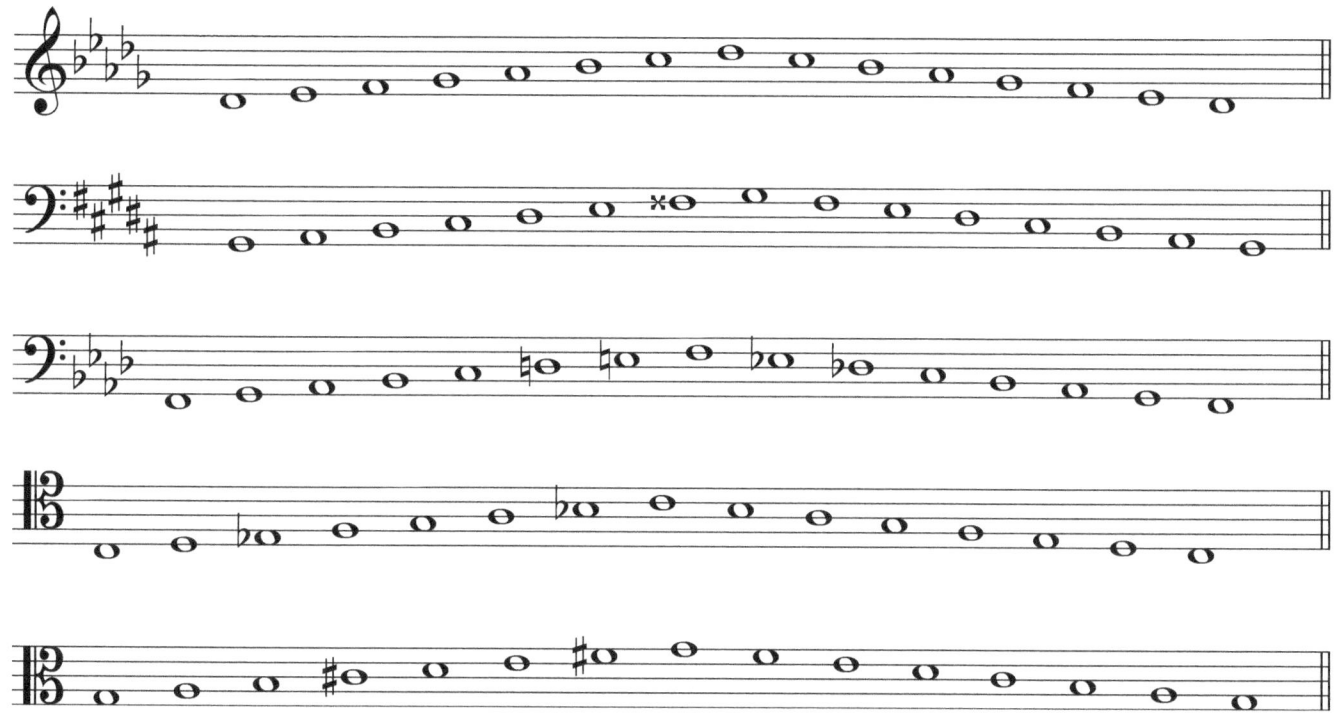

Page 114, No. 2

Page 115, No. 3

(a)   Ab minor   F# minor   G major   Bb major   Gb major
(b)   root pos.   1st inv.   2nd inv.   3rd inv.   1st inv

Page 115, No. 4

min 6   maj 10   dim 7   dim 3   per 5

maj 3   min 6   aug 2   aug 6   per 4

Page 115, No. 5

Advanced

Page 116, No. 6

Page 116, No. 7

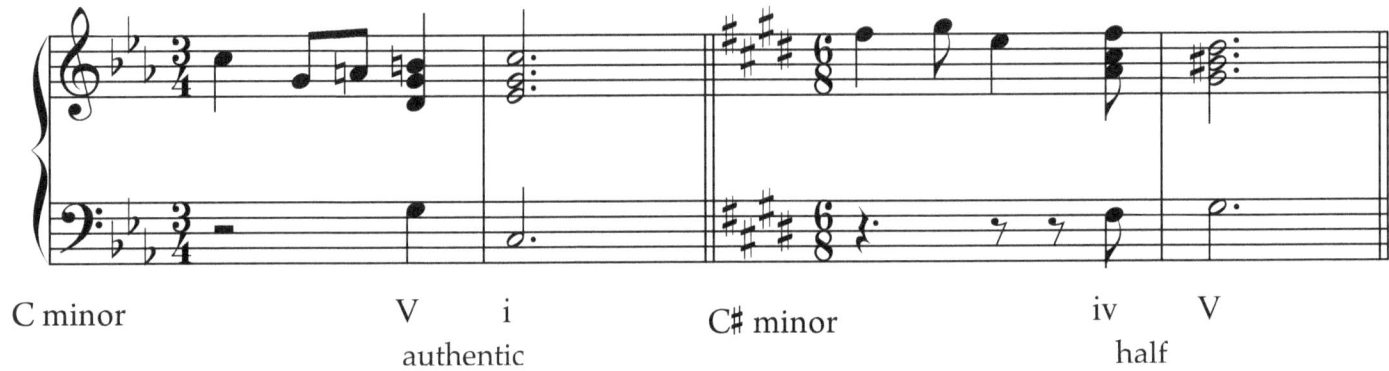

C minor   V   i   C# minor   iv   V
                 authentic   half

Page 117, No. 8

Johann Sebastian Bach

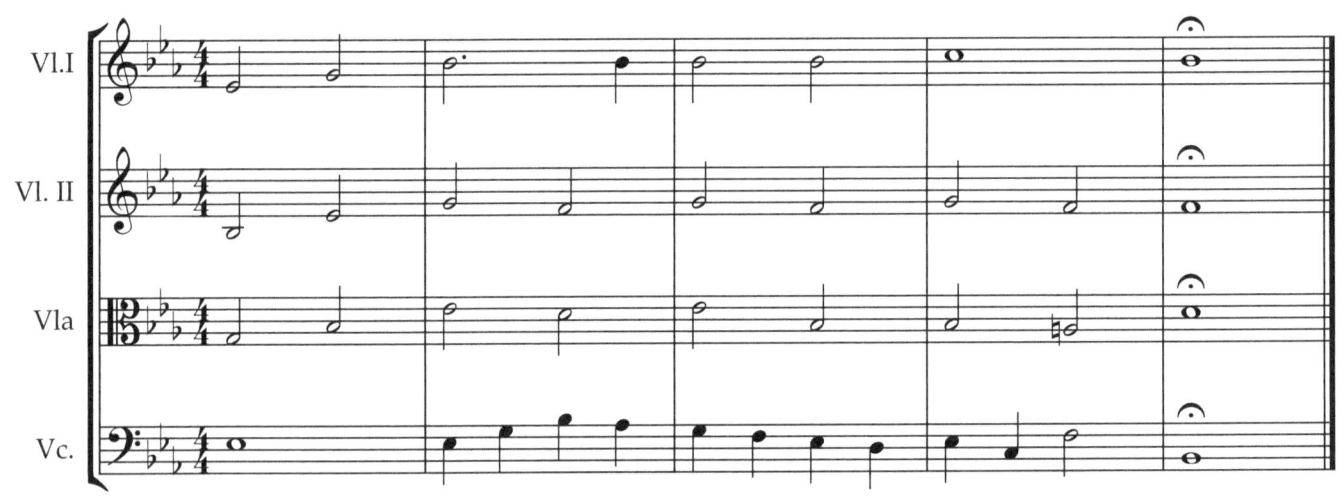

Page 117, No. 9

9/8   5/4   3/2   4/4   12/16

Advanced

Page 118, No. 10

(a) Write the time signature directly on the music. 3/4

(b) Name the composer of this excerpt: Friedrich Kuhlau

(c) Name the key of this excerpt: B♭ major

(d) Classify the chords at:

    A: root: B♭   type: major   position: root pos.

    B: root: F   type: dom 7th   position: 1st inv.

    C: root: F   type: dom 7th   position: 3rd inv..

(e) Name the intervals at D: min 3   E: min 7

(f) Circle and label one harmonic minor sixth in the excerpt. m.6 D to B♭

(g) Define *andante con espressione*.

    moderately slowly, with expression

Page 139

a) When did the Romantic era occur? **1825 - 1900**

b) Music that has a literary or pictorial association is called **program music**

c) Name two Romantic period composers. **Franz Schubert, Frédéric Chopin, Franz Liszt, Robert Schumann, Johannes Brahms, Felix Mendelssohn, Edvard Grieg, Piotr Ilyich Tchaikovsky, Guisseppe Verdi, Georges Bizet**

d) Where was Felix Mendelssohn born? **Germany**

e) Whose music did Mendelssohn help revive? **J.S. Bach's**

f) What genre is Overture to a Midsummer Nights Dream? **Concert overture**

g) What author wrote the play that this work is based upon? **Shakespeare**

h) What is the form of Overture to a Midsummer Nights Dream? **Sonata form**

i) Name the three main sections in this form. **Exposition, Development, Recapitulation**

Advanced

Page 139

F, F, T, T, F, F, T, T

Page 140

Petrushka
Composer: Igor Stravinsky Genre: Ballet

Koko
Composer: Duke Ellington Genre: 12 bar blues

Dripsody
Composer: Hugh LeCaine Genre: electronic music

Etude Op. 10, No. 12 'Revolutionary'
Composer: Frédéric Chopin   Genre: solo piano piece

Overture to a Midsummer Nights Dream
Composer: Felix Mendelssohn   Genre: concert overture

Page 140

Dripsody	Hugh Le Caine	Modern
Revolutionary Etude	Frédéric Chopin	Romantic
Koko	Duke Ellington	Modern
Overture to a Midsummer Nights Dream	Felix Mendelssohn	Romantic
Petrushka	Igor Stravinsky	Modern

Advanced

www.ingramcontent.com/pod-product-compliance
Lightning Source LLC
Chambersburg PA
CBHW081710100526
44590CB00022B/3719